Understanding The RV Park Business Model

Tyron .G Drummond

All rights reserved. Copyright © 2023 Tyron .G Drummond

COPYRIGHT © 2023 Tyron .G Drummond

All rights reserved.

No part of this book must be reproduced, stored in a retrieval system, or shared by any means, electronic, mechanical, photocopying, recording, or otherwise, without written permission from the publisher.

Every precaution has been taken in the preparation of this book; still the publisher and author assume no responsibility for errors or omissions. Nor do they assume any liability for damages resulting from the use of the information contained herein.

Legal Notice:

This book is copyright protected and is only meant for your individual use. You are not allowed to amend, distribute, sell, use, quote or paraphrase any of its part without the written consent of the author or publisher.

Introduction

This is a comprehensive resource designed to provide aspiring RV park owners and investors with the knowledge and guidance needed to succeed in the RV park, mobile home, and campground industry. This guide covers various aspects of starting, managing, and growing an RV park business.

The guide begins by highlighting the significant reasons to consider starting an RV park business. It explores the financial opportunities and potential for profitability within the industry, setting the stage for readers to understand the advantages of this business venture.

To get started in the RV park business, the guide delves into the financial aspects, offering insights into the investment required, funding sources, and financial projections. Readers will gain a clear understanding of the financial commitments and potential returns associated with RV park investments.

Understanding the legal and regulatory aspects is crucial in this industry, and the guide covers topics such as zoning, land acquisition, and the necessary licenses and permits. It provides valuable information on navigating these legal requirements to ensure a smooth and compliant start to an RV park business.

Types of RV parks and setting policies and rules are essential considerations, and the guide offers guidance on these matters. It helps readers define the nature of their RV park, whether it's an upscale resort or a family-friendly campground, and how to establish rules and policies that create a positive experience for guests.

Building, preparing, and launching an RV park is a significant undertaking, and this guide provides a comprehensive overview of the process. From selecting the right location and infrastructure planning to park layout and construction, readers will find valuable insights to help them successfully launch their RV park.

The first few weeks of operation are crucial for any RV park, and the guide offers guidance on these initial stages. It covers topics such as setting up reservations, managing guest arrivals, and ensuring a smooth start to operations.

Operating an RV park involves various aspects, and the guide explores them in detail. It includes information on managing day-to-day operations, maintaining facilities, and providing exceptional customer service to ensure guest satisfaction.

Marketing and advertising play a vital role in attracting guests to an RV park, and the guide provides a mastery of these aspects. It includes strategies for effective marketing campaigns, online presence, and customer engagement to maximize occupancy rates.

The guide also outlines the features and amenities that contribute to the success of campgrounds. It highlights the key factors that make a campground stand out and attract guests, ensuring a positive experience for visitors.

For those looking to expand their RV park business or invest in more parks, the guide offers insights into taking the business to the next level. It covers strategies for expansion, diversification, and continued growth within the industry.

In conclusion, this book serves as a comprehensive and informative resource for individuals interested in entering the RV park, mobile home, and campground business. It equips readers with the knowledge, tools, and strategies needed to thrive in this industry and create successful RV park ventures.

Contents

Chapter 1 – Big Reasons to Start an RV Park 1

Chapter 2 - The Financials 7

Chapter 3 - What You'll Need to Get Started 17

Chapter 4 - Zoning, Land & Licenses 27

Chapter 5 - Types of Parks and Setting Your Policies/Rules 37

Chapter 6 - Building, Preparing, & Launching your RV Park! 49

Chapter 7 – The First Few Weeks of Your RV Park 58

Chapter 8 - Operating Your RV Park 64

Chapter 9 - Marketing & Advertising Mastery 72

Chapter 10 - Features of The Most Successful Campgrounds 82

Chapter 11 – Taking it to the Next Level, Expanding to More Parks, & More! 88

Chapter 1 – Big Reasons to Start an RV Park

"The way to develop self-confidence is to do the thing you fear and get a record of successful experiences behind you. Destiny is not a matter of chance, it is a matter of choice; it is not a thing to be waited for, it is a thing to be achieved."

~ William Jennings Bryan

Investing in new avenues is a scary step, and in the case of RV Parks, also a time-intensive and full-commitment journey. Unlike passive investments like investing in stocks and other forms of real estate, the beauty of RV Park investing is that it is an active investment. It calls for you to learn something new about the world of travel, real estate investing, and even people's temperaments. Your decision to invest in an RV Park will impact more than your financial standing. More so if you plan to be an active part of the business, involved in the day-to-day activities needed to keep the park alive and sturdy. Every year, more and more people jump into the world of Recreational Vehicles, and since 2006, RV sellers have been selling more and more units to first-timers and veterans looking to upgrade their old RVs. With 10,000 people turning 65 every year, more and more retirees are casting out into the world now that they have time to do so. Traveling can be costly, and RVs allow retirees to travel cross country without breaking the bank on accommodation costs. With statistics predicting that the number of people turning 65 will double by 2050, it figures that there will be an influx of people considering RV Parks a viable accommodation option. Financially, this makes RV Parks a great bet, especially if the park provides its tenants with top-notch service that makes the stay memorable.

So, why is RV Park investing a **better option** compared to other real estate investment options?

• If you are looking to supplement your income or for a change in careers, owning a park allows you to do both. With RV Parks averaging a 10-20 percent return on investment, or $50,000 to $90,000 annually, becoming an RV Park owner gives you the chance to make a living and earn a modest income. Granted, this figure does not hold for all parks, but it gives you a chance to exercise your business acumen and find ways to improve the park's profitability through various means, including introducing new and upgrading existing amenities, improving services, revamping the park, and upgrading utilities.

The park's profitability is contingent upon many factors, but no matter what type of park you own or its amenities, management is the most significant contributor to its success. So, even as you embark on your park ownership journey, ensure that the management is not undermining your efforts. If you plan on being a passive owner, ensure that you take time to hire the right talent and keep yourself apprised of the ins and outs of the park.

• If you plan on being an active owner, the RV Park becomes your job, your security. For as long as you own the park, you are assured that you have a job and source of income. Since you are in charge, you get to set your working hours, granting you the freedom of being your own boss. While delegating tasks and diving into the nitty gritty details of everyday decision-making may be stressful, understanding that your income is derived from your efforts can prove satisfying. With job security quickly becoming a thing of the past, your park becomes the evidence of your dedication, the anchor that keeps you grounded in a world filled with uncertainties.

If your park is seasonal, being your own boss accords you the freedom to take time off when business is slow or low. With this time, you get to undertake other projects that you feel will be beneficial to the park, and to you as an owner, business person, manager, and human being.

- As an active owner, you get to live on the park property, a cost-saving measure that you will always appreciate. With the financing on the park covering your premises, you are not burdened with debt obligations of two different properties. Since you won't be paying rent and property taxes are on the park, you can enjoy better tax advantages in addition to the convenient accommodation arrangement. By setting up your abode within the park, the everyday expenses tied to commuting, mortgages, and living are sufficiently cut down. This means that even if the park is making a decent amount of money, you get to save most of it, allowing you to build a nest egg to help with future capital expenses or your children's college costs.

- Compared to other accommodation businesses like hotels and motels, an RV Park is less hassle in terms of maintenance and scope of responsibility. This translates to less operational costs, usually around 10% lower than hotels and motels. Your return on investment is much higher, especially if your park has a high occupancy rate.

Unlike hotels and motels, unless the tenants go on a rampage and actively damage the hookups or items in the common rooms, the damages sustained in an RV Park are minimal. Hotels and motels have walls, appliances, carpets, and furniture that can be destroyed, which makes repairs costly. With RV Parks, however, the tenants are in their own RVs, and any damage sustained is their responsibility. Also, with RV Parks, most inconveniences are caused by tenants damaging the landscaping, littering, or damaging hookups. These are pretty contained, so repairs are not bound to be too costly. Also, RV Park owners only have to maintain the lots, hookups, and utilities, which is considerably less work since it doesn't involve cleaning after guests and providing provisions in every room.

- The park resources - roads, sewer lines, water lines, electrical poles, etc. - have increased depreciation rates, which offers RV Park investors a significant tax benefit, allowing them to keep more of the income generated by the park.

- Socially, owning an RV Park allows the owner to connect with a wide array of people, allowing them to forge connections that might come in handy down the road. RV Park tenants come from different backgrounds, and if you take the time to strike up conversations with them, you get to discover new things, including what you can do to improve the park. A friendly owner is more likely to receive honest feedback, allowing you to fix any issues and improve their quality of stay, increasing the chances of the tenants returning or recommending the park to other people.

In most cases, the tenants will look to you, the owner, to guide them during their stay. Because of this, it is best to keep apprised of places they can go and things they can do during their stay. Which is the best restaurant in town? Where are they likely to find child-friendly activities? By becoming a sort of guide to your tenants, they get to enjoy a better stay, solidifying their view of the park. The park owner becomes a core part of their experience, which gives you the word-of-mouth advertisement that is known to bolster so many businesses.

Overall, a park is great for your social needs as a human being and your business through the connections you forge and foster.

- Unlike other hospitality businesses, the RV Park industry has mainly been recession resistant. Case and point; the COVID-19 pandemic. As businesses closed down and many hotels and motels reported low occupancy rates because of the lockdowns, many people were getting antsy staying indoors. RVs became the safe travel option, as they allowed people to keep their distance. With RV Parks giving them some level of privacy and excellent accommodation without having to interact with other people in close quarters, occupancy in RV Parks went up. Additionally, RV Park tenants are mainly retired and semi-retired people and individuals whose incomes allow them to ride the ups and downs of the economy. This means that RV Parks occupancy levels remain high even through hard economic times.

• Because of the barriers to entry into the RV Park business - getting all the zoning, local, and state requirements can be pretty difficult, and the lengthy time from construction to initial occupancy - competition is limited. This allows your business to maximize profitability with little fear of someone else launching another park nearby. And for as long as you provide impeccable services to your tenants, you will remain the preferred park for many of your customers, even if a new park happens to spring up.

• Because RV's can be driven off the park in just a few minutes, evacuation in case of an emergency is relatively simple, and any loss sustained will remain minimal compared to brick-and-mortar establishments. The repair costs will also be low compared to other permanent buildings, allowing your business to bounce back in a short time.

• If you plan to remain invested in the park business long term, you get to give your family a chance to be involved in a functioning business that can also sustain them in the future. This makes the RV Park a fun, exciting, and profitable family endeavor.

• Perhaps the best reason to start an RV Park is because of the readily available exit strategy - the land. Land is always in demand, and the land your park is on is a great asset that can be traded if you need to exit the business. In most cases, the land is even more profitable than the RV Park business.

For potential RV Park owners and investors, the benefits of diving into this business are immense, and they come in both monetary and non-monetary forms. When you dedicate yourself to the business and ensure that your customers have a memorable and enjoyable stay, you build the business through referrals. Also, building your online presence allows them to easily share your information, casting a wider net into a pool of potential tenants.

However, if your intention for entering this business is purely monetary, I'd advise against doing it. The RV Park business requires dedication to providing top-notch service, and focusing on the money creates instances where some expenses are cut, depriving customers of the wonderful experience they are used to. For example, the pool may seem costly because only a few visitors use it. However, you may lose many more customers if it falls into disrepair. Most people like having *the possibility* of indulging in a certain service, even though they may not necessarily use it. Replacing beautiful foliage with walkways and concrete paths may incur less landscaping costs, but the stark coldness of concrete may drive away many clients who like the look and feel of a beautiful landscape and the connection to nature.

Also, as an owner, you have to be open to criticism and willing to incorporate other people's ideas. Running the park with an iron fist will leave guests unwilling to make suggestions, and your employees are unlikely to pass on any complaints and recommendations they get from guests because they know it is futile. You may be the final decision maker, but the park runs best on teamwork. If you are a control freak who thinks they are always right, a different investment option may be better for you.

And finally, don't get into the RV Park business if you have no desire to run the park or if you despise working outdoors.

Chapter 2 - The Financials

"Diligence is the mother of good fortune."

~ Benjamin Disraeli

No matter who you are, what you do, and what you are aspiring towards, there's no denying that success is relative. We chase our ideas of success each day, setting milestones and targets that only we can explain and rationalize. The world of RV Investing is no different.

What makes a park or campground successful? This question will elicit different responses from different parties, all of whom are involved in the RV park and campground business. Hell, even investors have marginally different ideas of what makes the park successful. Some investors have their eyeballs glued to the numbers, choosing to find ways of cutting costs and increasing income to raise their profit ceiling no matter what. Others focus on reinvesting in the park and improving amenities to increase the camp's value, customer satisfaction, and long-term profitability. Some investors are focused on revamping and reselling, while others plan on making the camp their entire life, willing to sacrifice as much as possible to keep it running. However, no matter your motivation or metrics of success, the numbers matter. No matter how much you love and enjoy your work, it's bound to take a toll if profit margins are dismal or you're making losses.

In February 2021, Shenandoah Acres was revealed to be part of Sun Communities, Inc.'s portfolio, just a year after it had acquired new owners, SA Holding Co. LLC. However, many were not focused on why it changed hands. Instead, eyes were firmly glued to the whopping $17 million price tag. The greatest part of this story is that

SA Holding Co. LLC had only paid $3 million for the same park. What justified the $14 million markup for Sun Communities, Inc.? Originally a 280-acre property, Shenandoah Acres was launched in the 1930s by Rupert and Helen Blacka, and it remained in the family until 2005, when the Blacka family sold it to Good Faith LLC. The camp had undergone various changes and upgrades since its inception, but had been operating on and off for years. Once it was off the family's hands, this was the start of a decade-long hiatus for the campground. With rising insurance costs, Good Faith LLC chose not to reopen the park to the public, and instead had various management use the facilities. Finally, under the management of Garland Eutsler and Carolynn Rubino, Shenandoah Acres reopened in 2014. However, it wasn't long before the park changed hands again, this time for $2.4 million in 2017. Shenacres Realty took over the 134-acre property for three years before selling it to SA Holding Co. LLC for $3 million in 2020. How was Shenacres Realty only able to secure a $600,000 marked-up valuation in three years, and SA Holding $14 million in just a year?

This story stands out because it is an outlier. It is a testament to how chance favors the prepared mind. We may never know the details behind SA Holding's decision to buy Shenandoah Acres, but we can surely theorize. And theories have abounded in the RV space. My favorite so far is that SA Holding saw opportunities that Shenacres Realty was blind to. After all, with a land and property valuation of $1.8 million, how did a company with a depth of history in the RV and campground world find it fiscally justifiable to shell out $15.2 million for a property's intangible assets? The answer lies in the numbers.

As an aspiring RV park investor, your focus should never stray far from the numbers on your books. Success is multi-faceted, but in the business world, reputation and numbers are your greatest allies. While none of us may never see the record returns SA Holdings snagged in just a year, we still have a chance to make our mark in our own way.

Many parks have seen an uptick in income as more people look for cheap and affordable accommodation options for short- and long-term stays. In August 2020, RV manufacturers and sellers saw a 17.3% increase in sales compared to August 2019. As of April 2022, wholesale RV shipments are 10.1% higher compared to 2021. The rise in RV sales was initially attributed to people's need to avoid interacting with many people during the COVID-19 pandemic. However, it became clear that the rising cost of living and the need for cheaper travel and accommodation options also fueled the rapid growth in the RV industry. For some RV park owners, this period has been one of unprecedented growth, while for others, it has been a source of great distress. As more people join the RV lifestyle and park reservations rise, park owners have more work, more expenses, longer working hours, and, depending on the guests, unprecedented problems. Increasing income doesn't always translate to higher profit margins. Maximizing profits requires understanding your park's needs and optimizing staff and facilities to handle them with little need for repairs or replacements. It means keeping up with the finer details of the provided services and ensuring consistency in maintaining both the lots and shared facilities.

Also, all the administrative needs must be taken care of promptly and with little fuss. Are your licenses up to date? Are you conversant with the zoning, insurance, safety, and other legal issues pertaining to your park? Who is handling these for you? Do you have a proper audit process in place? Cutting costs by finding cheap services may seem like a good move, but fees and penalties have been known to bring businesses to their knees. RV park expenses vary depending on the type of park, and it goes without saying that primitive parks have the least expenses. However, the income is also minimal, and there is only so much that can be done to increase revenue streams in primitive parks.

The average profit margin for RV parks is about 10 ~ 20%, but this is not guaranteed. For many successful parks, the road to profitability was not straightforward and assured. Providing water and electricity may have been enough in the 90s, but even with partial hookups, park residents have started expecting internet connections as well. Your park's profit depends on your ability to satisfy your clientele so they become repeat customers, attract new customers, recruit and keep key staff members, and keep improving the park to optimize expenses and generate alternative forms of income.

The cost of starting a park is as dynamic as the profit margin. First and foremost, you have to determine whether you want to buy an already existing park or a barren parcel of land. Where do you want the park to be located? Do you have a location in mind, or are you willing to take the best deal? Whichever choice you make, you still have to choose the right location for the kind of park you'd want to run. If the park is near an attraction site or a highly populated area, the price per acre will be higher than that of a park located in a more remote location. Also, real estate prices differ from state to state, and you need to factor this into your budget. After choosing the location, determine what kind of park you want to run - will it be a primitive park, partially developed, or fully developed? Are you planning to provide additional amenities for the customers? What structures do you need to accommodate these services, how will maintenance run, and are there laws or codes that must be adhered to? The price of parks ranges from a few hundred thousand to millions.

You can usually justify the price of a park using one of three methods: the income approach, the cost approach, and the sales comparison approach.

- **The Income Approach:** A park's Profit and Loss statement is a great way to determine your expected earnings if you continue running the park in the same way. However, taking a deep dive into the statement will probably highlight areas that need changes to be made, which will either cost or save money. Once you have a pretty good idea about the park's gross income, its value should be about three to five times this figure.

- **The Cost Approach:** For all intent and purpose, this approach is usually the owner's way of recouping the money spent on improving and upgrading the park, the sunk costs, if you will. For the buyer, however, the value of the property has no such monetary attachment, as the past is just that. Have the owner's sunk costs translated into an increase in income, or did the bets fail? If the Profit and Loss statements don't show any change in income generation after the changes, the owner waged the wrong bets.

If this is the case, look into other properties for sale, or renegotiate the price to find a more realistic price

- **The Sales Comparison Approach:** This means that the park's value has been set using metrics pertaining to how other parks in the area are valued, the location's real estate prices, and the general value of other properties in the area. This method is flawed because it doesn't account for the park's expenses, upkeep, maintenance, and income. However, it provides a great starting point that helps determine your potential budget.

As you set your budget, remember that it is about more than the price of the park. Due diligence before signing on the dotted line will save your ass down the line. Gerry's park gave me a false sense of comfort that I followed that with decisions that make me cringe every time I remember them. Four years into running the park, someone approached me with what seemed like a great deal. They were running a park that had consolidated lots from three different purchases. Initially, the park was just a 12-lot partially developed investment with all-year-round occupancy. With the increasing occupancy rates, they had approached the owner of an adjacent property and paid 8% above market value. With the lot expanded to 34, things went well for a while. Then, the occupancy rates ballooned again and they approached the owner of the next adjacent land (or so they told me).

I checked the Profit and Loss statements, tax returns, and licenses, and everything seemed above board. All I needed to do was buy a portion of the expanded area as a partial owner since it was intended for longer-term stays. However, my $75,000 investment became a nightmare when the property owner moved back from New York a few months later and found the RV Park had illegally encroached on his property. Turns out that the person we were dealing with was a real estate agent who'd only been authorized to lease the property to residential dwellers and not for commercial purposes. All the expansion projects had to halt, and we spent more money fixing what we'd "destroyed" on the property.

Even if you hire experts to review the documents you've received from any potential seller, always ensure you have a good grasp of what is happening. As a buyer, your only focus should be on what you get out of the deal.

You've made up your mind and are sure you want to get your own RV Park. There's a problem, though, **you need financing** to make it happen. As a newbie in the RV Park business, obtaining conventional financing can prove difficult because you lack experience or the track record to prove that the business will be profitable under your control. You pose a significant risk for the financial institution, and if the underwriter or loan officer doesn't understand the RV Park business, your application has a greater likelihood of being rejected. Despite the potential challenges you may face, here are some **financing options** available to you:

- **Seller Financing:** This nontraditional lending is an excellent option for a first-time park owner as it allows you to avoid the red tape of traditional lending and gives you a chance to secure funding at great rates. With seller financing, you get to come up with a payment structure that will work for both you and the seller, with balloon payments curated to fit your unique needs. For both the seller and buyer, there is a certain comfort provided by this financing option. Both parties are secure in their belief in the park's value, which is reflected in the ensuing promissory note.

However, this financing option still poses a risk to both parties, and it is advisable that you find a real estate attorney with experience in seller financing to help you understand the sales contract, promissory note, and other legal issues pertaining to the sale.

Seller financing is popular because it involves fewer hassles compared to conventional borrowing, and often, it ends with both parties walking away with greater gains because of the saved costs. However, you will have to pay a down payment, so you better be prepared to negotiate with everything you've got. Also, ensure that there are no issues with property ownership, such as a mortgage or tax liens. Realtor Jason Burkholder of Lancaster firm Weichert advises: "Most mortgages have a 'due on sale' clause that prohibits the seller from selling the home without paying off the mortgage. So if a seller does owner financing and the mortgage company finds out, it will consider the home 'sold' and demand immediate payment of the debt in full, which allows the lender to foreclose."

As part of your due diligence, hire experts to help you navigate this financing option to avoid complications down the road.

- **SBA Loans:** Established in 1953, the Small Business Administration is a government agency responsible for providing small businesses with access to capital, advocacy, entrepreneurial development, and government contracting. However, the agency's loan guarantee program is what SBA is known for. Under this program, SBA guarantees a percentage of the loan disbursed to qualified small business owners.

SBA 7(a) loan is designed to meet the unique needs of small business owners in certain industries. This loan is commonly geared towards funding the purchase of land or building new facilities; purchasing existing businesses; repairing business capital or refinancing a debt; or purchasing furniture, machinery, equipment, technology, or supplies.

SBA 504 loans are also one of the most common SBA elements, but unlike SBA 7(a) loans, they cannot be used to repair credit, consolidate debt, repay debt, or refinance debt. SBA 504 loans are also known as Certified Development Company (CDC) loans, and are geared towards more specific purposes, like purchasing or expanding an existing business; purchasing land; converting or upgrading existing facilities; or purchasing utilities, parking lots, and other improvements specifically for park growth.

Because of their flexible rates, low fees, and low down payment, SBA loans are great financing options. However, obtaining an SBA loan is a lengthy and slow process, although it may be worth the try if no other option is working out. Apply for an SBA loan through an SBA-approved lender, making sure that you satisfy all the eligibility criteria.

- **Bank/Conventional Financing:** Obtaining bank financing for an RV Park is not a walk in the park, especially if you are a first-time owner. Most lending institutions will not consider your loan application if you do not meet their eligibility criteria, so it is best to be well-prepared if you plan on taking this route. The bank will perform its due diligence by researching the borrower (you), so take a deep dive into your financial history - credit rating, credit report, and financial statements - business experience (if any), and your business experience in real estate and RV Parks in particular.

As you look to secure funding for the RV Park from a bank, don't just settle for any institution. Finding an underwriter and loan officer with experience lending to RV Parks and real estate is the best option, as they will better understand the risks involved in this business. Once you have identified the financial institution, concentrate on finding its loan guidelines and customize your loan request to fit within the guidelines. If you're a first-time RV Park owner, your business proposal can give you the edge you need to convince the loan officer, so don't rush it. Make sure that your business proposal and loan application are well-curated to give you a chance to secure funding.

- **Conduit Financing:** This is perhaps among the complex forms of financing, as it involves using a third party to handle the details of securing the loan. However, this financing option features more documentation and loan costs and can be a pretty frustrating experience. While the rates may also seem attractive, the penalties may be unforgiving.

- **USDA Loans:** This is one of the less-known financing options, and its eligibility criteria are very confining. First and foremost, your RV Park has to be in an area that the United States Department of Agriculture (USDA) deems a rural area. To check whether the park is eligible for this loan, visit http://eligibility.sc.egov.usda.gov/eligibility/welcomeAction.do and enter the park's address and zip code.

If eligible, prepare for a fairly lengthy process since you'll be dealing with the USDA and bank. However, this is worth it if other financing options are not working out.

- **Others:** There are numerous financing options available, including hard money lenders, mortgage brokers, private money lenders, and life companies. You can also use your credit cards, although this is a fairly risky option that may destroy your credit rating, so you better be confident in your ability to pay back. A business line of credit will be a good fallback option during the low season, but you need to avoid relying on this too much.

Choosing a financing option may be a complex process, but don't give up hope, and always choose the option that fits your needs.

Chapter 3 - What You'll Need to Get Started

"You find that you can have the best business in the most exciting industry, but if the execution, if the torch-holder, if the value-creator isn't there, then we don't make it happen."

~ Dan Levitan

Location. Location. Location. This business term has been drilled into our psyche since time immemorial, and for good reason. The San Francisco Bay Area is expensive, but any startup tech company with dreams of making it has a better chance of success if they are based in Silicon Valley. The access provided in this region is invaluable, and many tech bros realize this. And as with all things business, your RV Park business is not exempted from this rule unless you have a really niche idea. So, how do you **choose a location** that is great for your business's success?

First, focus on what kind of park you want to run and the amenities you wish to provide. If you want to launch a survivalist-type camp, a remote area deep in the woods will work wonders. Your guests will have an authentic experience, and you get to keep the land undeveloped for as long as the park remains a primitive one. For luxury camps and "glamping" destinations, a remote location might not be ideal. You may get away with setting it up in a rural area, but the park still needs to be near an urban center with various attractions and access to specific services and activities. For family-themed parks, amenities and activities need to be provided to keep the families engaged and willing to revisit the park. There are numerous considerations to make, but these all depend on your vision for the park.

Once this is determined, you can choose **where** you want the park to be located. Some states have more RV Parks than others, with Texas, California, Utah, Montana, and Arizona boasting the highest number of parks and Hawaii having nearly none. You may see this and think, "I'll start an RV Park in Hawaii." This would be a stupid idea.

If you're starting your RV Park investment journey, dig a little deeper and find out why some states have more RV Parks than others. California is a destination state, and RV Parks are great for guests who need affordable accommodation as they visit the various sights and indulge in the activities. Utah, Montana, and Arizona boast incredible sights and nature's wonders, providing great incentives for people to visit. RV Parks in remote and semi-remote areas are successful because they cater to weary travelers looking to rest for a night or two before getting back on the road. These parks are usually just off the road for easy access, and have just enough amenities to keep guests comfortable. Do your due diligence. Once you find your ideal location, you still have another decision.

Raw land or established park?

We can argue for and against either choice all day long, but the decision ultimately lies with you. For most investors and business owners, **building a new park** offers various perks: you get to design the park as you see fit, install amenities following the recommended guidelines and adhering to applicable laws and codes, create a brand, and overall control over what goes where and how things are created. Buying raw land may also seem cheaper, as it's devoid of any development. However, when you choose this route, you have to consider a few basic facts.

- **Phase One Environmental Study:** This report is generated to help the seller and/or buyer evaluate their liability. By researching whether there are issues with the soil and existing buildings that could threaten the environment or the public's safety, you determine if the property's value is what it is purported to be. While you may be inclined to trust the seller's assurances that there is nothing wrong with the land, I'd suggest leaning toward caution. If the report comes clean, you rest assured that you will not be met with fines or be liable for any damages in the future.

However, if the report uncovers contamination on the property, you get to avoid thousands in cleanup costs or a better deal for the property.

- **Park Layout and Acreage:** So, how many acres do I need to purchase? There really isn't a right or wrong answer to this question. First, you need to check the local laws. Some municipalities limit how many RV lots can be situated on an acre. Also, if you plan to franchise, there may be guidelines on how many campsites you need per acre, or in total, guiding the size of land you need to purchase.

The park layout/plan will also determine how much land you need. If you plan on going private, you need to consider the size of the lots, the general design of the park, the layout, how much privacy you'll accord the customers, the parking style, buildings, sewer system, etc. For a franchise, you will be provided with plans that you have to adhere to. Whichever option you take will dictate how many campsites you need to be profitable, and the acreage. Additionally, some municipalities limit the size of an RV Park, so make sure that you look into this also.

- **Landscape:** What's your vision for the park? Are you planning to cut down any trees or integrating the campsites within the trees? Are you planning on creating a more streamlined landscape with hedges, fences, and paths lined with well-crafted grass? Do you plan on building on a hilly area or flat ground? Your campsite environment is more than just the paved ways and well-lined parking sites. You need to determine how it all fits in together with your vision.

A primitive camp will feature minimal human interference, but glamping and resort campsites need to have concrete plans outlined, especially pertaining to design and maintenance.

- **Infrastructures and Amenities:** Which buildings do you need? Will there be an on-site house and/or dorm for the staff and manager/owner? Where will this be located? Where will your septic leach field be? Garbage disposal area? Are you planning to dig wells or get connected to the supply line? How about electricity, WIFI, etc.? Who will install these features? Because your site will be devoid of any development, you need to carefully consider your planning and the placement of every infrastructure in the park.

A good commercial contractor with experience building RV Parks will be a valuable asset, and you should reach out to other park owners for advice. Their expertise will be invaluable in helping you avoid common pitfalls. Also, ensure that you obtain the proper permits and licenses before commencing any development to ensure compliance and avoid expensive fees and penalties.

- **Construction Costs:** Who is going to handle construction? Are you handy, or will everything be outsourced? Once you have obtained the necessary building permits and approvals, the next step is to build the park. Whether you are doing the work yourself or need to hire a construction company, ensure that you are aware of everything going on. Check the billables and ensure that the company is not cutting corners. If possible, get quotes from multiple companies and the proposed timelines. Additionally, budget for inspection costs if you are not conversant with building codes or construction details.

To be safe, set aside a windfall amount (5-10% of the quoted amount) to help you cover the costs of any unforeseen problems. Also, ensure you obtain the proper permits for signage directing campers to the park. These should be constructed following the municipality's guidelines.

If your plan is to **acquire an established park**, here are some considerations you need to make:

- **Income:** This is a no-brainer. Through the profit and loss statement, you get a general idea of how much the park is bringing in annually. Additionally, you need to check which part of the business is bringing in what amount of income. For example, if the park has a convenience store, a laundry service, and/or other attractions or add-on services, establish which brings in the highest income and the least.

Also, be aware that not all owners or managers record the amount of money received, so make sure to ask whether there is income that isn't put on the books. This will help you determine how much is really coming in and help you streamline the business to avoid tax liability.

- **Operating Expenses:** How much is spent on keeping the park up and running? These expenses include utilities, salaries, payment to contractors, permits and licenses, maintenance of equipment, repairs, insurance, etc. As you review these expenses, find out if the owner/management has listed personal expenses as business expenses. For example, if the owner uses the business income to fuel and maintain their car on personal trips, payments for personal entertainment, etc. Also, check which expenses were capital expenses so that you can account for maintenance expenses in the next financial cycle.

- **Other Expenses:** What other expenses have you identified that do not contribute to the running of the business? For example, refunds, contributions, emergency expenses, etc. These may not be recurrent or unrelated to the business, but you need to detail them to determine if they can be slashed.

- **Insurance and Risk Cover:** What is the scope of the current insurance cover on the park? How protected is the park? Is the coverage sufficient or will you need to update it? Are the workers covered? If not, why? If workers are covered, how comprehensive is the coverage? By understanding the insurance and risk cover, you get to determine if this is sufficient to protect you from liability, and how much it will cost if you decide to expand the cover.

- **State of Amenities:** Are the buildings, lots, equipment, and amenities in good working order? Are they in disrepair? What needs repair and proper maintenance? What requires replacement? Will the cost of making these repairs be covered by the seller or will they be deducted from the buying price?

- **Capital Improvements:** Is there new equipment that needs to be bought? New buildings? Is there capacity to construct new campsites, or do the sites need new paving and upgrades to adhere to new standards? Some capital improvements may be clear from the get-go, but others may need you to be more familiar with the camp to notice. Because of this, I'd suggest spending a few days at the park observing everything and using every available facility.

- **Sewer Plant Records and Readings:** The sewer system can be a source of great headache if it has any problems you didn't notice before purchase. Determine whether the sewer plant and system has ever been inspected. If it has, when was the last inspection? Check the reports and call the inspector if possible. Replacing sewer systems can be expensive, and if it is not a budgeted expense, it can redirect funds that could have been used for other income-generating services.

Ensure that the sewer system is well maintained and functioning properly. If not, you can use this to renegotiate the price of the park or adjust your budget.

- **Existing Surveys and Environmental Reports:** Since the park is already up and running, you may assume that there may be no environmental risks. However, it is always a great idea to ensure that there is no risk. Ask for the recent survey and environmental reports, if any. If the property has never had an inspection/study, schedule one or ask the owner to do so. This allows you to determine if the value is as quoted, if there may have been issues caused by the constructions, or if there are existing risks posed by how the park has been operating.

Waste disposal and sewer systems can pose great risks if they are not handled or operating properly, and you may want to avoid liability. Also, is the water supply uncontaminated? Are the pipes functioning properly? Are there any leaks? Are the electric poles well maintained, and is the electric supply well-grounded? Inspections will give you peace of mind and ensure that you don't find yourself with a property that needs more overhauling than was planned.

- **Utility Meter Readings, Records, and Formulas:** Utility costs make up a significant chunk of operating expenses, and it is great if you understand how the charges are determined. By checking historical records, you get to compare the utility costs over time. This will help reveal if any issues cause spikes in expenses, like increased capacity or leaks.

- **Personal Property (Transfers Upon Closing):** Is there any personal property used in the business? For example, the owner may be using his personal truck to run the business, or a few personal RVs for customers who don't own an RV but want to experience the park. Some tools and equipment owned by the owner may be used in the business to keep costs down. In many parks I've owned, I usually used my truck and construction equipment in the business to bring down expenses.

In many instances, I moved with the property but left a list for the new owners. You can negotiate to keep some equipment, or ask for a list of properties included in the sale.

- **Permanent Occupants:** Does the park have any permanent tenants? If it does, first confirm whether this is legal in that jurisdiction. If legal, obtain a list with details about the tenants. How long have they been in the park? How much do they pay? Which services are they entitled to? Also, find out if there are tenants who pay rent late, have any special needs, or are generally a headache to deal with. Is the rent from these tenants included in the books? Do they pay for repairs? Can their lots be moved if they are in prime lots?

These details give you an idea of how to approach or deal with these tenants. Also, the tenants themselves can be a trove of information about the running of the park and any issues, especially long-term issues, that have yet to be addressed.

- **Owner's Experience and Specialized Knowledge:** I attribute most of my success to the fact that I am pretty handy, so I could keep the cost of revamping and running campgrounds relatively low. My wife was also a great asset as she handled most of the restocking and administrative duties. Because of our input (and the fact that we lived in the parks), we were able to handle most of the repairs and administrative duties while only taking a small portion of the profits. If the owner or park's manager has been handling repairs, the cost of running the campground will be lower. This is also true if they live in the park, as they don't need to pay for another property.

If you are not handy, it is best to realize that the cost of running the camp will increase because of the outsourced work. This is also true if you're not planning to live in the park. Ask the owner for a list of repairs they handle, and factor this in the expense sheet, accounting for adjusted rates depending on the contractors you plan to hire.

- **List of Contractors and Service Providers:** Which company handles waste disposal? Who handles repairs and any work not undertaken by the staff? Who are the suppliers or distributors? Getting a list of the contractors who work at the park will save you time trying to find contacts when you need work done. This list is valuable, so check in with the listed contacts and find out their rates and the type of work they do at the park.

These considerations are just the tip of the iceberg, and ultimately, it is up to you to decide which option serves your needs best. However, if you are just getting into the business of RV Parks, my two cents is that you find an established park and use it to learn more about parks. This way, by the time you choose to build your own park, you will have a wealth of knowledge that will help you create a park that you love and that has a great chance of succeeding.

The value of the competition

Scoping the competition is an absolute must, no matter what investment you want to make. With RV Park investing, scoping the competition (both successful and struggling parks) is a way to gather more information about running your park. Start with parks in the area you are interested in, as they are your direct competitors. What amenities do they have? What kind of park is it? How many employees are there? What advertisement platforms do they use? Are the facilities efficient or in disrepair? What about the camp was most satisfactory? What could be made better?

By compiling a list of things to look for, you get to highlight things that your park may need, and things that can be done away with. However, your mission does not end here. Once you've scoped local campgrounds, it's time to cast the net a bit wider. Which parks are making waves? Visit these parks and stay for a few days to get firsthand experience. With parks located further away, it is better to visit the more successful parks. During your visit, strike up conversations with other people, but don't be too pushy or keep asking questions. Let conversations flow, and take every opportunity to talk to the owner or management. While not all will be willing to talk to future competitors, many are more than willing to share their knowledge.

This connection with other park owners is invaluable as they can help you get great deals, reveal issues with your planned purchase, or even help you avoid hiring contractors who do substandard work. Additionally, the value of other parks in the area gives you a ballpark of the true value of the park you are looking to buy, or what you can hope to bring in once your park is completed. When it comes to your RV Park business, **the competition is not always a bad thing.**

Chapter 4 - Zoning, Land & Licenses

"If I have all of the gear but I can't bait the hook, the fish have nothing to worry about."

~ **Craig D. Lounsbrough**

After taking time to consider your options, you've decided that you want to create a park that fits the image you have in mind. You are willing to take the time to develop an RV park and work to build your clientele from scratch, despite the challenges that pave the way. I am an impatient person, so this route has never suited me. Additionally, I love seeing myself work on an existing park and convert it into something utterly unbelievable. Despite shying away from raw land and lots, I have helped several people who've chosen this route, and there are some things that you cannot afford to skimp on.

One owner, let's call him Jeff, decided to get land in rural Florida for a small RV park dedicated to outdoor enthusiasts. He planned to partner with a tour company so guests could opt in for various activities at an extra charge. He had a plot of land he was eyeing, owned by one of his distant relatives. Believing that his family had no issues that would hinder the sale, he bought the land after doing a cursory appraisal to ensure he was paying the fair value. The land was previously part of a ranch and had abandoned mobile homes scattered all over the property. In four months, the deal was complete, and Jeff was the owner of a plot of land. Or so he thought. After handing over a considerable amount of money to his relative, Jeff finally got a real estate lawyer to perform a title search. The relative was not the sole property owner, and he had no authority to sell it.

Additionally, there was an outstanding fine from the local council because of the abandoned mobile homes, which had been deemed dangerous. This was six years ago. Jeff is still fighting a legal battle with his relatives because of the property, and he's become a pariah because he was accused of trying to steal land from family. While he still went ahead and bought a different park, he still regrets his decision to trust someone so implicitly in a business deal. He has never recouped the money he paid for that property, and he was forced to heavily finance his next investment.

My advice? Don't be like Jeff. There is no place for implicit trust in business, and you must do your due diligence.

Now, back to the main focus. You have identified the perfect **plot of land** for your RV Park, and you are afraid someone else will scoop it up if you don't act fast. While this may be true, especially if it is a prime plot of land, don't let impatience cloud your judgment. Real estate investing is a delicate and complex process, and you don't want to be left with property that is of no value to you and that you cannot sell without incurring heavy losses. Before bidding on the property, you need to do your due diligence and collect as much information about the property as you possibly can. The more information you get, the better. Here are a few things that you should never overlook:

- **Appraisals:** Is the property fairly valued? An appraisal is an excellent way to determine if the land is worth the quoted price. Is the price too high above the market average, or is it too low? While an appraisal is usually one of the most important things, some sellers don't take the time to do it. Before making an offer, ask about the last appraisal. If there was a recent appraisal, review the report. If none was done, make it a contingency for buying the property, or you can choose to get an independent appraisal done out-of-pocket.

Whichever option you take, ensure the proper appraisal is done by a qualified real estate expert.

- **Inspection:** Since you will be creating a space where people will be staying, you have to ensure that there are no potential dangers and that the property is viable for installing necessary amenities. Is the property near the municipality utility supply, or will you need to find ways of supplying the necessary utilities? Is there a possibility of digging a water well to provide safe and clean water? Do you need to independently install power lines? Is there enough space for a septic system and a sufficient leach field? How about access to the property, right of way to the neighbor's property, gate installations, and accessibility? etc.?

For you, this inspection needs to be diligently carried out by an inspector with experience in the RV Park industry. While you may have your list of things to look for, someone with expertise is more likely to check things that you may not have considered. To be safe, do not skip the inspection or take the buyer's word that an inspection was undertaken.

- **Survey:** A survey aims to confirm the property/boundary lines. The survey will help you ensure that you are not encroaching on the neighbor's property and they are not encroaching on yours. Sometimes, unknowingly, the property boundaries provided by the seller may be erroneous, and you have to ensure that you do not get caught in the crossfire if any legal issues arise.

- **Contingencies:** What about the land diminishes its value? Through the inspection, survey, and appraisal, you may discover issues with the property, like problems with the right of way, supply lines, wetlands, etc. These issues will likely bring up the cost of your development and make a great bargaining tool. For example, if the septic system needs to be repaired or replaced, factoring in this cost as a contingency can help bring down the cost of the property.

However, you need to ensure that these contingencies are put on paper and worded correctly. These contingencies can give you an out if you change your mind or find a better property. Do not try to create these contingencies yourself. Find a real estate attorney to draft your agreement with the contingencies.

- **Clear Title:** There's nothing worse than finding yourself saddled with legal issues and complications after paying for a property. A "clear title" just means that the property is free of encumbrances like legal issues or liens and that the seller is authorized to sell the property. A clear title means that once the property is transferred to you, it is yours, free and clear. Your attorney is responsible for carrying out a title search and giving you a heads-up if there are any issues with the property. While land records may not always be 100% accurate, you save yourself the hassle by ensuring you've done your due diligence.

- **Legal Representation:** While you need to have legal representation when closing your deal with the seller, a real estate attorney is a valuable asset **before** you make an offer. If you find a real estate attorney with experience dealing with open land, you will have a greater advantage than just hiring a general real estate attorney. Once you hire your attorney, make sure you are honest about your plan for the property. This way, they can include the relevant contingencies to your purchase and sale agreement. Your attorney will also better structure your deal with the proper contingencies to give you an escape hatch if you ever feel the need to back out of the purchase.

In addition to wording your contingencies in ways that protect your interest, your attorney will also provide proper escrow management to protect your money in case the property fails to meet your standards or is deemed insufficient for your development plans. Your attorney will also help you with the title search and any issues pertaining to the deed, deed restrictions, or zoning issues that may affect your development project.

But before you get excited and make your plans, you must ensure that an RV Park is a viable development on the plot of land you are eyeing. **Zoning maps and ordinances** dictate what is allowed within a specific area. Permitted land use is not about denying individuals the right to undertake whatever project they have in mind. Rather, zoning maps and ordinances distinguish different land uses, ensuring that incompatible land uses are not located adjacent. The ordinances also fortify the city's safety and resilience by setting limitations on buildings and land use. The zoning maps and ordinances can dictate lot sizes, density or bulk, building height, and floor area ratio. Because zoning maps and ordinances need to be adhered to, you need to check if the land you're looking at can be converted into an RV Park. Checking the area's zoning is as simple as heading to the relevant government office; this can be the mayor's office, city attorney, department of housing, or even the public library. In some areas, the homeowner's association will also have the relevant materials. The zoning laws commonly include; noise restrictions, building restrictions, animal and pet restrictions, and trash and refuse. Some cities have zoning maps and ordinances posted online for easy access, so ensure that you look into this also.

Even if you're buying **an existing park**, you need to review the zoning ordinances to establish whether the RV park conforms to the laws. The owner may have gotten away with it, but this may not be the case for you. Also, you may buy a park with grand schemes of expansion or adding buildings and services. Zoning ordinances may restrict new development, so you need to review the ordinance and ensure that your plans are per the outlined laws. By ensuring everything is being handled properly, you spare yourself the risk of losing your business, or you save yourself from buying a property that will land you in legal trouble.

The ordinances may be incomprehensible because of the language and terms used. If you need help interpreting the ordinances, visit the city or county Planning and Building Department. Or, if you can, find a real estate lawyer to help you understand the laws. A lawyer may be a better bet because you get to share your plans for the area, and they will advise you on what's permitted and what's not permitted. All in all, legal representation is essential even if you don't get to buy the property.

In addition to complying with zoning laws, ensure that you have the **necessary permits** to seamlessly run the park. The number of permits you need varies depending on the facilities in the park, but here are a few standard permits:

- **Employer Identification Number:** This is a must-have for any business for tax purposes, and you cannot operate a business without this. If you are building your park from scratch, you need to obtain the EIN even if you do not have any employees. For an existing park, the EIN can be transferred to you since it identifies that specific business. However, ensure you update the details if you make any pertinent changes to the business.

- **Special Recreation Permits:** Does the park have activities open to guests? If there are activities, including those that involve nature, like lakes, ponds, or trails, you need to obtain a special recreation permit. Research which permits are required for each activity to ensure you acquire the proper permit. This will help you even as you get insurance and reduce your liability if anything happens.

- **Drinking Water Facility Approval:** Water wells, treatment plans, and water supply systems are all for public consumption, and safety is paramount. This facility approval can last the facility's lifetime, but you may need extra permits if you need to change the system, upgrade the system, or add any modifications to improve supply.

- **Live Entertainment and Music Permit:** Even if you're not planning on hosting bands on the campground, having this permit is an excellent investment if you ever need to entertain your guests. Poolside entertainment, music in the common halls, and even movie nights can be great for your guests, and having the right permit is a no-brainer.

- **Health Permit:** Will you serve your guests food and drinks? Are your water supply and septic systems safe? Health permits vary, and you should take a deep dive to find out which health permit you need for the facilities within the camp.

- **Sign Permit:** No matter how beautiful your signage is, ensure that it complies with the county or municipality's requirements. There are laws dictating signs' size, placement, and lighting, so ensure you obtain the proper permit to display your sign. You may need to part with a few dollars to put up the sign, and in some areas, this fee may be recurring.

- **Restaurant Equipment Authorization:** Are you planning to set up a restaurant within the park? If so, obtain the right authorization before installing the equipment to ensure compliance.

- **Pool Operator Certificate:** Who will be manning the pool? Who is in charge of the pool and the relevant services? Whoever you hire should have the necessary permits and certificates.

- **Campground License:** This is a must-have for any RV park or campground which exceeds a certain number of occupants. The stipulations for this license vary from state to state, so ensure that you have complied with the set regulations.

- **Swimming Pool Permit:** This should be obtained before constructing the pool, as each state has specifications about how pools should be built.

...and many more.

The above list by no means exhausts the number of permits you may need to take out to keep the park running. Always do the necessary research and due diligence to ensure you are not overlooking something. The penalties you may incur because of non-compliance can cut into your profits or even jeopardize your park's existence.

Insurance and Risk Management

This is probably a no-brainer for you. Every business requires insurance, right? While the answer is obvious, it is easy to choose the wrong insurance for your business and end up on the losing side if anything goes wrong. I've experienced enough insurance payout headaches that I now prefer paying exorbitant prices instead of hoping for the best. My first advice if you're looking for insurance for your RV Park: look past the cost. When I got the first park, I looked through the Profit and Loss statement and decided to go with whatever cover Gerry had for the property. However, after his kids sold his truck and a few equipment, I discovered that I'd been paying the insurance premiums for some of Gerry's equipment and his widow's health insurance. I'm happy it only took a few months to discover this, and I made the necessary adjustments. However, a year into owning the property, one RV owned by the park was damaged by a small fire. That was when I discovered how dismal the park insurance coverage was. Gerry had only taken out a property coverage policy that did not cover the RVs and cabins on the property, including my residence and the spaces occupied by employees. I had to revamp the cover, and in the end, I chose a different insurance company.

Since then, I have always taken out two major covers for any RV Parks I own:

• **Loss of Income Coverage:** This is a great cover as it covers part of the lost income whenever something happens. In one instance, guests trashed one of the family cabins in a park I partially owned in Georgia. As we focused on repairs and cleaning up the cabin, the insurance company paid out 80% of the projected rent based on the previous rental information. While we still had to charge the guests for the damage, the insurance payout helped us carry out the repairs as we waited for the payment from the guests.

However, always ensure that you read the fine print on this coverage. Some companies only pay out for a few months or until the repairs are complete, not until occupancy. Also, check the fine print to see under which circumstances coverage does not apply. One park owner found out the hard way that their loss of income coverage did not apply if a guest caused the damage. In this scenario, the guest had accidentally hit the lot hookup, which rendered the lot unoccupied for a few weeks during the peak season.

• **Property Coverage:** When getting property coverage, imagine what could happen during a disaster. What would get destroyed? This way, you can create a list of things you want to insure. Imagine taking out property coverage, and after a tornado, you discover that the electric poles in the park are not covered by your insurance. The out-of-pocket costs for these repairs are substantial, and paying a higher premium would have resulted in less hassle.

Your insurance costs will be determined by the "extras" you choose and the facilities being insured. Swimming pools, fences, utility systems, and other amenities may require insurance, but this will be an added cost on top of the basic insurance. As you shop for an insurance company, look for one with experience dealing with RV Parks. These insurance agents will understand the business and the risks and liabilities posed. To determine if the agent is familiar with the business, ask questions and check the fine print to ensure that their answers are correct. There are many times when I have been told that something is covered, only to check the fine print and find that this was not the case. As with everything else, do your due diligence, be patient, and don't let the dollar signs cloud your judgment.

Chapter 5 - Types of Parks and Setting Your Policies/Rules

"You never know when your life is about to change. You never know when one decision will dramatically impact your life and change the course of your destiny."

~ Dani Johnson

It bears repeating that not all parks are the same, and you need to understand how RV park categorization goes beyond the amenities, facilities, and hookups provided. While the general purpose of every park is to provide the residents with a satisfactory stay (no matter how long it is), the work that goes into ensuring top-notch service is dictated, at its core, by the type of park you are running. Granted, there will be overlaps, and few parks are exclusively one type. You need to identify your business niche and work on maximizing its potential in terms of income and impeccable service.

Overnight RV Parks

These parks usually offer a short reprieve for travelers, as they accommodate RV owners for a night or two. Overnight RV Parks are created to be comfortable rest areas for tired drivers heading somewhere else or who may need a safe place to regroup before going back on the road.

These parks can be primitive, partially, or fully developed. However, their most notable features are location and signage. Overnight RV Parks are usually located near the road, and their signs are well-lit, conspicuous, and usually just a few miles from the park itself. The park may be on a long stretch of highway with minimal development, and serve to give drivers a chance to rest in a relatively safe place. Because of the nature of the stays, these parks are not facility-intensive, and services usually include basic cleaning and repairs.

If your prospective park is an overnight RV park, your focus should be on providing efficient services around the clock because drivers will be in and out of the park at all times. A well-stocked convenience store with nonperishables may be a great idea, and you can diversify by providing reliable parking to other vehicles if you have the space.

Short Stay RV Parks

These parks are destinations in themselves, as RV owners book accommodation for the length of their stay in the area. However, these parks limit the length of time a guest can stay, stipulated by either the park's rules or by local ordinances. Because guests can stay for a relatively extended period, these RV parks can be amenity-intensive to ensure that guests have everything they need on-site, plus a few extras.

Restaurants, shops, laundry, swimming pools, and other recreational activities can be provided to help keep the guests busy and content. Short-stay RV parks are relatively easy to maintain, as the focus is on keeping amenities well-maintained and ready for use at designated times.

Extended Stay RV Parks

These RV parks host guests for months, and they may also have permanent residents. Extended stay RV parks are particularly popular with people who like staying put, but still love moving from one place to another. Retirees also choose extended stay RV parks as it allows them to settle in a place for a while and move on when it's time, without committing to a home.

With these parks, it is best to provide privacy to the guests, and this can be done by providing private bathrooms and well-fenced lots. Restaurants, dining halls, laundry, convenience stores, and other entertainment amenities or activities are great additions to these parks. They give guests the convenience they need, allowing them to remain in the park without needing constant provision runs out of the park.

Seasonal RV Parks

Migration is not exclusive to birds. Texas parks are great places to migrate to when winter hits hard, and some parks have evolved to accommodate the migrating guests. However, high occupancy is not limited to harsh weather seasons. Other seasonal parks are popular during various holidays or when there is an activity that draws crowds to the area.

With seasonal parks, you should have information on the best places the guests can visit, a list of activities, and a general guide on how to enjoy their stay in the area. By including activities in the park and various attractions, the park maximizes income during high occupancy periods.

Like all other seasonal businesses, the number of employees at the park will be higher during the busy seasons, which makes staffing a crucial part of the management's duty. You have to determine which employees will remain on the payroll throughout the year and how to procure temporary workers during the busy periods. To ensure that your guests enjoy quality time at the park every season, set yourself apart as a great employer to keep the invaluable workers coming back to the park.

Destination Overnight RV Parks

Areas frequented by tourists will always have demand for accommodation, and RV park owners are not immune to the call of niche tourist spots. With destination overnight RV parks, the parks offer accommodation to guests visiting the area, and may also have perks like itineraries and guided tours to the best spots in the area, or just information about the best times to visit, which activities to partake in, etc.

Because guests are in the area to have a good time, the park needs to be cozy enough to keep the guests comfortable while also offering entertainment options like pools, games, and activities to keep kids and families occupied. Bonfires, video game centers, and pool games are great options, and the park needs to be sufficiently staffed to ensure that guests are always attended to. Such parks may also have park-owned RVs and cabins to rent out to non-RVers, to give them a chance to enjoy the amenities and experience RV living.

Destination Resort RV Parks

Destination resort RV parks differ from destination RV parks in that the resort park **IS** the main attraction. Guests come specifically because of the amenities and features of these parks, which may include niche activities that the guests are interested in. Amusement parks, petting zoos, rides, niche games, and other activities are the backbone of the park, allowing guests to remain in the park while still indulging in fun activities. These parks have great dining options, shopping experiences, and a host of activities to choose from.

Because of the broad range of activities, this park is not great for an owner without prior experience in the industry. Staffing demands are greater than any other park, and with so many moving parts, the park requires intense involvement and excellent management practices to ensure that everything is safe for the guests, and that the accommodation aspect is well run to keep guests coming back.

Membership RV Parks

RV owners essentially buy a membership that allows them to stay at eligible parks at discounted rates or for free for a set amount of time. An RV park owner may join the clubs offering memberships to attract frequent guests to the facility. However, you need to ensure that joining these programs will not hurt your bottom line.

Franchise Parks

Kampgrounds of America (KOA), Yogi Bear's Jellystone Park Camp-Resorts, Thousand Trails, Good Sam, Sun Outdoors, etc., are just a few franchises available in the RV Park and campground world. Buying a franchised camp or choosing to franchise your new development can be a great option because of the brand reputation you gain. With franchises, however, you don't have much freedom in many decisions, as you have to abide by the franchise's rules, which dictate the park's size, design, services, and staffing. You are also liable to pay franchise fees yearly, no matter how your business fared.

If you don't mind the lack of creative freedom and just want to operate the park in an already-established model, this is a great option. However, if you are building a new park, make sure that the local ordinances and franchise rules align.

...and many more

The above is by no means exhaustive, and when you factor in the option of overlapping services, things can get even more complex. For example, all RV parks fall under the three major categories - primitive, partially developed, and fully developed. Additionally, one park can offer primitive and partially developed options for its guests.

When buying or building a park, you have to consider the services offered to determine what this means for the park's management. A destination resort park will have more staff, many of whom will need to specialize in different aspects of the park. Emphasis will be on staff members trained to repair the machines in the amusement park, for example, and safety staff. This is marginally different from employees in a destination resort park, as they only need to take care of the guests' needs. Activities can also be outsourced to keep costs down. Additionally, more activities on the campground affect your insurance rates and call for higher safety standards to avoid liability in case of damages or injury.

As a first-time RV park investor, it is best to start simple so you can gain the necessary experience to find footing in the more complex RV park operations.

Campground Pricing Systems

How much should you charge your guests? This is an important question because accommodation fees are the bulk of your income, with any other services being extra. Regarding pricing, various factors will affect how high - or low - your rates will be. This, in turn, will influence whether you charge a fixed or dynamic fee.

- **Seasons:** There will be seasons when the occupancy is higher than others. With this in mind, you need to structure your fee in a way that helps you cover your expenses during these periods. High occupancy translates to higher operation costs, as you need more employees, greater security, and frequent waste disposal. Also, consumption of water and electricity will be higher.

- **Location:** This goes without saying. Parks with great natural attractions and views, or fun activities to indulge in, will attract more guests. Because of the demand, you have to ensure that the price sufficiently reflects the quality of the stay. Beachside and lakeside properties cannot be compared to parks in remote areas, and those in prime cities and areas frequented by tourists will always have higher demand.

Additionally, parks in areas with high living costs, higher taxes, or higher utility rates have to offload these costs to the guests, resulting in higher rates. Therefore, the location of your park greatly determines how much your guests need to pay.

- **Number of guests and/or pets:** While it would be ideal for guests to bring as many people as they can, this is not financially feasible. Pets require areas for exercise, which need to be maintained. Additionally, more guests in a lot mean higher water and electricity consumption. Therefore, it is best to clearly state how many guests the base price covers, and include extra charges for every additional person - child or adult. Pets can also incur extra charges, and the amount is at your discretion.

- **Amenities:** Electricity, water, waste, WIFI, air conditioning, laundry, cable, etc., all contribute to the guests' stay, and you need to factor in these costs in your final bill. Will you use coin laundries or include laundry as an optional service in the accommodation fee?

Is air conditioning available in common areas? High-speed WIFI costs a pretty penny, and you have to determine if this will be included automatically or if it can be an extra service the guest can opt for.

- **Rig Size:** RVs are not all the same, and the rig size determines utility consumption, lot size, lot location, and parking complications. Because of this, you have to determine how to price your fees so that the guests pay a fair fee that encapsulates the needs of their vehicle. For example, a 50 amp rig is not comparable to a 30 amp rig for obvious reasons. So, why not charge each guest accordingly, so one does not bear the burden meant for someone else?

- **Additional vehicles:** How many extra cars can you allow per RV? If a family has one member driving the RV and others following in a second, third, or fourth car, how do you cater to their parking needs? How many cars are allowed per guest? Parking fees for extra vehicles is something you also need to determine since parking lots still need maintenance, which means that you will dedicate manpower to taking care of the lot as well as providing sufficient security by placing guards, surveillance cameras, and proper lighting. Anything that incurs expenses in the park needs a clear income stream and/or funding funnel.

Personally, I prefer a dynamic pricing system so that I can efficiently cover the needs of the park without compromising the guests' quality of stay. For cabin and RV renters, I usually have a fixed rate for high occupancy seasons since I already know how much work goes into these sections of the business. However, there are caps on the maximum number of guests and cars before the guests incur extra costs, whose rates are also fixed.

For RV owners, however, I found that fixed rates almost always lead to my incurring losses in one way or another. One park I bought had a fixed price system, but I never realized that the original owner had waste management as an extra service since these were never included in the financial books. After five months of posting losses, I had to revise every aspect of the business to find where I was bleeding money. To date, I have no clue why a full hookup plant had a different waste management charge.

Now, every park I have had the pleasure of owning has dynamic rates determined by season, lot size, rig size, lot location, number of guests, parking needs, and any extra services they may need. For long-term guests (more than ten days usually), I offer discounts and perks to make their stay worthwhile. These range from free laundry services and cable connection to offering free stays for a set number of days depending on how long they stay.

To set your rate, you can consider your competitors' rates and choose to match theirs or offer other perks to make your park more attractive for guests looking for value for their money. No matter which choice you make, you have to be clear about your pricing system. If your prices fluctuate too much, guests may avoid the park because they can't budget their stay. As with everything, the key is finding the right balance with your pricing system so no one loses.

Policies and Rules

Your park needs to be hospitable to every guest, which means implementing rules and policies to create a serene and comfortable environment. For many people, noise restriction is the most important rule. Guests need to relax and enjoy their stay, which is impossible if their neighbor is blasting music or hosting a rager in their lot. Also, drunken misbehavior is a no-no for many people, as drunk people are likely to cause damage and injury to others in the park. Weapons also rank high on the list of things that need to be restricted in the park.

As you consider your park's rules and policies, here are some of the common areas that need precise rules and policies dictating conduct:

- **Recreational vehicles (RVs):** The condition of the RVs needs to be considered, with some parks limiting the types and ages of RVs allowed in the park. For example, some consider RVs over ten years old to be safety hazards, so they are restricted to reduce the owner's risk.

Additionally, some parks have small lots, which limits the size of RVs that can fit. RVs with leaks or other issues may also be restricted. Essentially, it is up to the owner to decide which RVs can be hosted in the park.

- **Sites:** The sites are all curated for each guest's comfort, and it is up to the guest to ensure that they don't compromise the state of the site. The guest needs to keep the site clean and safe, which includes not storing things under the RV, keeping appliances in the RVs, and limiting what activities can be carried out on the site. Additionally, the guest has to respect their neighbor's site and keep to their side of the fence.

Specific rules pertaining to each site will differ depending on the park, so it's best to carry out research and determine which rules apply to your park.

- **Visitors:** You can't ban your guests from hosting visitors, but you can set rules regarding overnight guests, additional vehicles, and supervision of underage guests.

- **Pets:** Are pets allowed? If yes, which breeds are restricted? Are there off-leash spaces allowed? Essentially, these rules are meant to guide the guests on taking care of their pets while in the park and on which charges are incurred if they fail to adhere to the rules.

Pet-related rules are usually imposed to ensure the safety of other guests and staff, and to ensure guests clean up after their beloved pets.

- **Parking:** How many cars are allowed on the lot? Can guests park on the street or not? Providing detailed instructions about parking ensures that the park is not littered with random vehicles blocking paths or left on empty lots. Additionally, prohibiting driving through vacant lots and enforcing penalties keeps the guests in line.

- **Conduct:** Keeping guests in line requires enforcing rules that dictate which behaviors are acceptable and which are not. Which rules to enforce are at your disposal, but always ensure that the rules prioritize the safety of your staff and other guests.

- **Accessory equipment and structures:** What structures are allowed on sites? For example, you can allow some covers but restrict the sizes. Hanging lines, furniture, and other equipment can be allowed or restricted. For example, only outdoor furniture is allowed on the site, but there can be a limit on the number of items allowed to avoid clutter. Additionally, grills may be allowed sometimes, and restricted when there is a high fire risk.

- **Emergency and safety:** Emergency and safety rules need to be provided to every guest. This includes instructions on what to do in case of an emergency, safety procedures, and emergency contacts. Evacuation instructions also need to be included.

- **Personal vehicles and bicycles:** Parking and storage of personal vehicles and bicycles need to be stipulated. Is there a designated parking space for extra vehicles, or a safe storage area for bicycles? Which have the right of way on park roads?

- **Miscellaneous:** These rules include anything else you may think of. Repairing rigs in the parks may be allowed or restricted. Moving rigs after a certain period may be stipulated. Any rule you deem important and doesn't fall under any of the above categories can be highlighted here.

When setting your rules, remember to keep them sensible enough. And always be ready to deal with guests who question the rules provided or choose to ignore them. Clearly stipulating penalties ensures that the guests know the consequences of their actions. However, ensure that your rules are written in clear, concise language to avoid confusion.

Chapter 6 - Building, Preparing, & Launching your RV Park!

"You can't plow a field simply by turning it over in your mind."

~ **Gordon B. Hinckley**

If you decide to build your park from the ground up, you have your work cut out for you. In this section, we will assume that you've already purchased your parcel of land, and are gearing up to start construction. The first step is pretty obvious, but I will still go ahead and ask - **what is the state of the land?** Does the land have trees? Is it in a flood-prone area? What's the weather like in the area? How big is the parcel of land? What is the terrain like? Understanding the intricacies of the state of the parcel of land you have purchased allows you to determine if your dream plans will work out or if you need to restructure them to match the situation.

The closest I've come to constructing a new park was when my partners and I decided to redesign a Colorado park to get rid of the primitive campground and install a pavilion instead. The area featured shrubs, a simple porta potty, and a small crudely built outbuilding used for showering. With no plumbing, electric, or paved access, we were essentially starting from scratch, even though it was only an acre. Our first order of business? Creating an easier access road to the area. While the open field was great for those looking for a more rudimentary stay, we needed a better system since the area would be accessed by multiple RVs at a go. The goal was to have the lots set up in a semicircle and the personal cars parked in one corner of the area. With two group lots to start with, the project seemed simple enough. However, we were soon embroiled in heated discussions about the lot design because the initial plan would call for us to chop down a great deal of trees. While the plan to have pavilions would be great for the park, I was not for the idea of clearing too many trees. The park's ambiance and beauty were largely maintained by the abundance of trees, which included a few fruit trees. It was back to the drawing board.

This decision unleashed new problems because now we needed to create an entirely new entrance to the pavilion to bring down the cost. Additionally, the area was relatively hilly. While this was great for the privacy of the tented camps and a great off-road experience for some of our adventurous campers, we needed to flatten the area for the RVs that would camp at the pavilion. For the excavators, our decision to spare the trees proved to be a headache because they needed to dig manually in the areas the machinery couldn't access. The only reason we could keep the cost relatively low was because I signed a contract to let the excavators use some machinery that I already owned at no cost. By allowing them to use my construction company's machinery for a month whenever they needed, we saved about $70,000. The final product was magnificent, but the project was delayed by about five months because of our environmental priority.

On paper, your plan may seem simple enough, but it's not until the construction starts that you discover unprecedented problems that weren't evident before the excavation. My advice - involve the experts as soon as possible. This way, you get to understand how the complications will impact the total cost of the project.

For many RV park owners who create their park, the first order of business is usually laying out the roads. By digging and leveling the roads, - usually wide to allow for easy maneuvering of big rigs - you get to give the construction crew easy access to proposed lots so that construction moves quickly. In our park, we just dug out the road and held off on adding crushed rock and gravel. We knew we'd eventually pave the road, but this project was slated after we determined how successful the pavilions would be.

Once the road is laid, it's time to work on the lots and other outbuildings. Does the plan outline where the bathrooms, bathhouses, recreation centers, offices, and other buildings will be located? The placement of amenities can influence the price customers are willing to pay, as some lots will be considered more prime than others. For example, lots further away from bathrooms mean that guests will be more inconvenienced. Also, those closer to the canteens, pool, and recreational centers can have an easier time enjoying the amenities. So, you need to consider the placement of these buildings.

Additionally, some facilities need to be well separated to avoid contamination. Bathrooms and laundry rooms can be within the same vicinity, but this should not be the case for dining rooms. The placement of your septic tanks and leach fields, or water wells, have to be carefully considered also.

Budget Estimates

Numbers make things a lot clearer, and here I'll give rough estimates on what the park may cost to construct. However, make sure to do your diligence because these numbers may vary widely depending on where your proposed park will be, the contractors you use, and the varying licensing, insurance, and permit costs.

Land: I launched this chapter assuming that you've already chosen/bought land that you feel best fits your vision for your park. Just in case this is not the case, I will highlight how much you can expect to pay for an undeveloped piece of land. In some remote areas, the price can start as low as a few hundred dollars per acre, but these locations may be too remote for your guests to venture.

Generally, expect to shell out from at least $1,000 to $1,000,000 per acre. The price tag, expectedly, is determined by the location and access to amenities and natural resources.

Excavation and/or Clearance: The property's condition will determine if you need excavation, and if so, how deep? Leveling the plot of land is essential for the park, so you have to allow the experts to determine what needs to be done. If the terrain is relatively flat, the amount of work required will be marginally less. However, other construction in the park, like offices and outbuildings, may need proper excavation for the foundation, especially if you plan on constructing a multilevel structure. The cost of excavation varies depending on the method of excavation, depth of excavation, type of soil, distance and method of transporting excavated soil, water charges (if any), and the contractor's profit. To get an estimate for this, I'd suggest visiting some websites that provide free estimates or consulting a contractor who will understand the dynamics of your property.

Clearance will be needed if the property has trees, shrubbery, or other plants that may impede the construction. Clearance, for the most part, is usually determined by the density of the shrubbery and trees, and the national average for a heavily wooded area ranges from $3,150 to $5,030 per acre. However, this can vary significantly, and it's best to consult a contractor.

Other earthworks, such as digging trenches for cables and drainage, can be embarked on by the same teams if possible.

Roads: Road construction is a multi-step process that will rack up costs quickly depending on your needs. If the land has trees, clearing them for roads will not be as simple as cutting them down as you have to completely remove them, which will cost anywhere from $400 to $1,200 per tree, depending on the height and size. In addition to tree removal, you also need road clearance, which can be anywhere from $250 to $1,000 per acre. There are also costs for proper drainage, grading and re-sloping, materials, labor, and permits. The width and depth of the road also play a great role in the cost of the project, and for an RV park, the roads have to be sufficiently wide to allow easy rig maneuvering.

The materials you choose to use - gravel, concrete, or asphalt - also contribute to the overall cost of road construction. For a small park, gravel may be sufficient, but this becomes unsustainable for a large park with high occupancy. You need your guests to easily get in and out of the park. For asphalt, it may cost you $10 to $15 per square foot. Gravel can be cheaper, at about $5 per square foot, with stabilized gravel going as high as $15. Gravel is an excellent option in areas with no snow, and because it is easy to maintain, you may opt for this route initially. Concrete will cost you a pretty penny, going up to $20 per square foot. However, because of its durability, concrete can be a great option for high-occupancy parks.

Ensure that the drainage is properly installed, as pooling water in the roads will create problems that may be costly to fix.

Fencing: Protecting your guests is a no-brainer, and fences make this possible by preventing unauthorized access to the property, keeping off looters and other stragglers. You may choose different materials to fence your park, but the most common include - chainlink, wood, or vinyl. My favorite so far has been to use vinyl and then line the fence with foliage that partially covers the fence. While this is sometimes counterintuitive to the main reason I started using vinyl - to save money - I fell in love with the aesthetic. Wooden fences can look beautiful, especially when they are well-maintained and repainted before the paint chips get excessive. However, at an average cost of $17 to $45 per linear foot, the expense can be high for large properties. In addition to regular maintenance, the costs can really dig into your bottom line. A chain link fence is also a good option, and with a $15 to $40 price tag per linear foot, it's cheaper than wood. However, because of its susceptibility to rust, you have to be sure to paint it over regularly and constantly check for any areas that may be cut. In one of the primitive parks I owned early into my RV ownership career, I put up a chain link fence and grew climbing vines, which ultimately covered the fence and gave the park a nice rugged look. It also saved me from having to paint the fence. However, we had a few guests tumble into the fence and get scratched up, so signs were put up for their safety.

My favorite, vinyl, initially saved me money when one project had gone way over budget. I had a few employees who were able to chip in to install the fence in exchange for free board for a few months since they wanted to move out of their shared apartment in town. Because of the easy maintenance and relatively easy installation, I was hooked on using vinyl - well, until I discovered adding flora to the mix and landscaping costs became my burden to bear. Vinyl fencing can set you back $19 to $35 per linear foot, but the cost can go as high as $60. If you're not installing the fence yourself, please confirm the cost of the various fencing options with the construction team to determine which one will serve you best.

Supply Lines: The electric, water, and sewer supply lines are crucial for the park, and how they are run across the park will depend on the park's design, the location of the transformer, the well or water company's supply, and the septic tanks. When it comes to installing these utilities, consult the relevant experts so you can get a proper estimate of costs, which will vary because of your park's unique needs. Remember, these supply lines will still run through the outbuildings and any amenities added to the park that will be used by guests. As you get your estimate from the experts, don't just focus on the lots, but on everything in the park that may consume electricity, water, or need the sewer system.

Lots: A fully functional lot, with up-to-code supply, will cost anything from $15,000 to as high as $50,000. This figure varies because of the various decisions you make regarding the construction of the lot. Will you use gravel, concrete, or asphalt to line the lot? This will drive up or lower the cost. Adding private fire pits, bathrooms, or other "extra" features on the lots will drive up the cost considerably. For the power hookups, you need to factor in that RVs have different supply ratings, and including 50 amp, 30 amp, 15 amp, and 110/120 voltage outlets is the right thing to do so that your guests can connect power without any risk of harm.

Outbuildings: Constructing offices, public bathrooms, laundry rooms, pool houses, rec centers, and/or employee housing will also require proper planning so everything flows well. Constructing each outbuilding will typically cost around $20,000 for every building, but this does not factor in any special installations needed to get the rooms ready for their desired functions. A proper plan shared with the relevant contractor will give you a better estimate of what it will cost to build and get the building ready for use.

Permits: Before embarking on construction, ensure you obtain the necessary permits. The cost of each permit and/or license will vary from state and municipality, so make sure to carry out the necessary research into which ones you need. Also, there may be federal regulations that apply to your park, so ensure that you find a contractor with relevant experience in the RV park industry, as they will be a great source of information pertaining to what permits and licenses you need.

Others: Your park may include other amenities like park models, cabins, tiny homes, swimming pools, restaurants, WIFI, air conditioning, etc. Each will feature its own costs, require specific permits, and adhere to set codes. If you plan to add these amenities later after the park is up and running, ensure that you make this clear in your planning phase so that your contractors can advise you on the best way forward. It may be expensive if you later need to dig up supply lines because your initial planning did not factor in future expansion plans.

Marketing: Social media has been a great tool, as it has allowed businesses to market their services for a relatively lower price than traditional media marketing. If your park is part of a franchise, the corporate office will handle your marketing needs as outlined in the franchisee contract. However, as an owner of an independent park, you need to find ways to market your park to potential guests. You can partner with influencers in the RV niche, various RV sellers and resellers, use social media, billboards, etc. Whichever form of marketing you choose, ensure that you set aside enough funds for the marketing campaign, and that you provide impeccable service to your guests so that they become your champions too. Peer advertising is still one of the most effective marketing tools to date.

Market Research

Even if your park is the only one in the area, you still don't exist in a bubble. While RV park owners may have unique ways of operating their parks, there are underlying management techniques that can work across the board. Every so often, even as a park owner, I take some time off to visit some of the popular RV parks in and out of state. Sometimes I make it a family vacation when I'm going to family-themed parks, but for the most part, it's usually just Cheryl and me. We usually stay at a park for about a week, as this allows us to get acquainted with management, some of the employees, and other guests. The purpose of the visits - work and play. While we enjoy the time we spend in the parks, we also take note of the things that work well in the parks from the moment we are received to the moment we leave.

My most memorable stay was at a small park in Colorado. The booking process was simple, and we were given a code to input once we got to the main gate. The guard received us warmly and guided us to the main office, where an employee was already waiting with the relevant paperwork clipped to a board.

Once we'd filled out the forms, an employee on a dirt bike guided us to our designated lot, where he helped us park and hook up our RV. He explained the park's rules and gave us safety packets, a map of the park, relevant contacts, and complimentary snacks. He left once he had ensured we were okay. There was a small dining area, where you could bring your own food or call the office if you wanted to be included in the dinner list at an extra charge. When we got to the dining area - which was set up like a quaint beachside restaurant - we were escorted to our seats by an employee, and as we wrapped up our meal, the park owner came by to greet us.

The park had no pool, but every night there was an entertainment act set up either in the dining hall or the entertainment area, which featured lounge seats and an array of well-set-up fire pits. With WIFI, air conditioning, and laundry, the park was sufficient enough to keep us comfortable. There was no store on site, but there was always a grocery run done by an employee every morning, and all we had to do was hand out a list of what we needed, and we'd pay after they'd delivered the item(s). Needless to say, this was a great insight into what is possible even in a park with few extra amenities. The level of care and attention we got as guests trumped everything else. I spoke to other guests, and many confessed to coming back because of the hassle-free stay they were accorded every time.

There is no one way to run a park, so you need to be aware of how your peers in the industry are carving out a loyalty base for their parks. Also, you can visit parks that are not doing as well to find out what pitfalls you need to avoid in your park.

Chapter 7 – The First Few Weeks of Your RV Park

"June reared the bunch of flowers you carry from seeds of April's sowing."

~ **Robert Browning,** *The Patriot.*

Your park is now completed… what next? If your answer is "get guests pouring in," this may not be the right answer… **yet!** Once your park is completed, you need to perform a thorough test run - a beta test, if you will - to ensure that there are no issues with your amenities or lots. There are various ways of going about this, which include performing the tests yourself and tapping into the power of the local RV community. This beta test can also be a marketing tool for your new park to help you drum up future business. I first heard of this "beta test" concept eight years ago when I became a silent partner in a project involving an abandoned campground. A 30-something Silicon Valley executive, Aaron, was looking for a "pet project" and had somehow ended up connecting with one of my former partners in Colorado. Paul forwarded my number to Aaron, who was willing to drive up to Colorado for a meet. To say he'd done his homework was an understatement.

The park he was interested in had been built in the 70s, and it was a small mom-and-pop five-acre property that had fallen into disrepair. There were a few tenants in the area, but they had old RVs that were rusted out, and they couldn't afford to move them. The compound had also been littered with abandoned RVs and shelled-out cars, so it was more of a junkyard than anything else. I was appalled by the photos Aaron showed me, and immediately I began expressing my apologies. "I can't go into this with you…." I started. But Aaron wasn't taking no for an answer. He'd researched the relevant codes, contacted a company that would get rid of the junk, and already offered the tenants a "buyout" to get them to leave the property. He'd made sure to sign contracts with the owners. The deal - he would pay all the fines accrued on the property and pay them the balance of the asking price in cash. His grand plan - **gutting the entire park.** My experience in the RV park industry was telling me not to touch this deal with a ten-foot pole. I was afraid **of, and for,** Aaron. I was not sure how it would work out. I left that three-hour meeting with my mind made up. I was going to turn him down, even though he hadn't explained what my role would be in the park. As we crossed the parking lot to Aaron's car, I noticed that his attorney was inching closer toward me. He said goodbye first, shook my hand as he uttered the words: "Don't say no yet. Come to Florida first. There's always a method to Aaron's madness." I was baffled, but curious.

Three months later, I got to see the method in the madness. Aaron's idea of gutting was nothing I'd personally experienced before. He wasn't tearing it all down. Instead, he settled for restoring most of the outbuildings that were determined to be habitable. He'd gotten rid of the dumped RVs that were utterly useless, and most of the shelled-out cars. The rest, he'd put them in one corner of the park. The power cables were dug up, and so were the water pipes and septic tanks. Everything would be replaced and brought up to code. And so, this went on for about a year. I visited four more times, and I was left shell-shocked each time. There really was a method to the madness. Eighteen months after my first meeting with Aaron, he finally revealed that all he wanted me to do was manage the park for a 15% stake in the park. I wouldn't get a salary, but my accommodation and living expenses would be his responsibility. He just needed me to stay at the park for two years, and in that time, show him the ropes. I would also train a manager.

I was scared. Aaron was a force to reckon with, and I wasn't sure he would accept taking orders from me, someone who didn't take unnecessary risks. But he was adamant, and when Cheryl accepted moving to Florida, I was in. I joined in when the construction was wrapping up. Aaron had taken the abandoned RVs and turned them into cottages on wheels that could be pulled from their spots using trucks. The remaining shelled-out cars were turned into lounge spots in the entertainment center, which he dubbed "the essence" of the camp. Aaron envisioned creating a hub for people to work and still get some vacation time in. There was no pool, but he set up a bunch of soak-in ponds.

Six months after I had moved to Florida, he dropped the "beta testing" bombshell. He was set on opening the park four months after completion. I didn't understand it, but he assured me it was okay. First, he reached out to various RV lifestyle bloggers and offered them free accommodation for a week in exchange for honest reviews. He also spoke to other RV park owners and invited them to stay and share their opinion. Then, he did the strangest thing yet - he invited enough people to get the park to full capacity for a week. I balked at this. The guests were offered free accommodation and free rein of the facilities, except the laundry room. They would cater their own meals, drinks, and any entertainment charges. We were running wild for those four months. Each group's stay uncovered a bunch of issues, and we would scramble to have them all fixed. In the end, the park opened three months past the initial set date. Fortunately for us, we were an immediate hit.

Aaron's beta test had involved a diverse set of people, many of whom were happy to come and pay for their stay and to see what impact their reviews had on the park. Most of them were over the moon when they found that Aaron had turned some of their comments - bad and good - into a mural that spanned one side of the external office wall. Additionally, pictures of the initial guests were turned into wallpaper which covered one wall in the indoor rec center. I stayed in the park for four years before I decided to take a silent role. The park was sold six years after its opening, as Aaron got jittery and decided to chase a new dream.

Aaron's beta test was an extreme version, which was possible because he had enough disposable funds to make it possible. While you may be unable to give people free stays at your own camp, you still need to test if your park is ready for occupancy. You need to stay in an RV in the lots to check if the hookups are all working correctly. Invite other RV owners and offer them a major discount for helping you out. This way, you get a feel of how your system will handle a certain occupancy level. The contractors will have their own way of testing the systems, but you must do your due diligence. As you start, you need to create a system that will offer compensation in case the guests encounter issues with the amenities or hookups. This can be an extra day's stay for free, a complimentary meal, or a discounted stay the next time they stay at your park. A **soft opening** is also a great way to test your systems, discover potential problems, and have them sorted out before your official opening.

Listings

Having a website is a great way to set up a seamless booking system for your guests, but it will take a bit of time before your website ranks high in the search engines. If you are a franchisee, your booking systems will already be in place and running, courtesy of corporate. However, as an independent park owner, you need to employ a few different avenues so that your guests can book their stay simply and easily. If you have on-site model parks, cabins, or RVs, posting these on Airbnb and other rental websites is a great way to kickstart the stays before guests discover the perks of booking directly through your website. For RV owners, various campground listing sites cater to their needs, and adding your park to these sites can help drum up your business. Sites like rvonthego, outdoorsy, campspot, and spot2nite offer RV park owners the opportunity to list their parks for a fee.

However, offer a few perks to get guests to book through your site. This way, you get to save money on fees to other websites, and your guests are incentivized to keep using the official website.

Your First Guests…

As your park starts receiving guests - either during the beta test phase or after officially opening - you have to leave a lasting impression. In the service industry, "all attention is good attention" doesn't apply. You should always aim for positive attention, as this will build your reputation in the industry. The RV park community is inexplicably tied no matter what state the guests may hail from, and with many RV owners asking for their peers' recommendations on parks to stay in, your brand needs to have a positive response, or at least a neutral one. If you take over a park that was mismanaged, writing "under new management" does not magically wipe the guests' memories clean. You have to work for the change in opinion. It's akin to plugging the hole of a sinking boat before removing the water in the boat.

I have always greeted my guests and welcomed them to the park before handing them over to an employee to take care of their needs. This way, they can immediately put a face to the brand. When I am not busy running around dealing with the multitude of things on my to-do list, I am usually in the office admitting guests. I make a point of being at the office on weekends when most guests check in or leave. If I don't have the time, I attend some of the activities, usually with a few small gifts for the children in the park. By making the time to mingle with guests, I discovered I could learn more about what parts of the park weren't working.

So, as a new park owner, I urge you to make the time to get acquainted with the guests. Join the welcoming committee, and if you don't have enough employees yet, show the guests to their lot and check on them from time to time to ensure they are okay. Well-prepared information packets are also necessary, as guests feel they are being taken care of. Emergency contacts, the park's rules, and a little souvenir make great additions to the packets.

Now that your park is up and running, you may feel like you can relax. The hardest part is seemingly over, but this may not be the case. Many parks are brought to their knees by management problems, not lack of amenities or low occupancy. You spent every waking hour ensuring that the park was viable for business after construction or property transfer; you need to spend a few more waking hours ensuring that every part of the system performs optimally to ensure that your guests leave the park satisfied and yearning for another stay.

Chapter 8 - Operating Your RV Park

"I find that the harder I work, the more luck I seem to have."

~ Thomas Jefferson

A successful business, it seems, stems from a combination of luck, hard work, and the right decisions. For many successful people, however, luck seems to take away from the hard work they put into their trade and all the hardships they had to overcome. I believe luck has played a part in every success and failure I have experienced, and I look forward to every challenge posed by the projects I undertake - within reason, of course. The difference between successful and struggling parks may be clear sometimes, but for the most part, it's hard to tell what aspect of the business is not working out. After getting my first park out of the danger zone, I was excited to implement new things to increase the park's profitability. There really wasn't much to do, but I was determined to find something. For months, I visited the successful parks in the area, looking for "that" thing that would tip the scales in my favor. And after a while, I figured I'd gotten it.

Many of the parks I visited had activities the guests were urged to participate in. These included karaoke nights, game nights, and sometimes movie nights. I was excited. I'd had guests ask about our entertainment schedule, and telling them about the pool didn't seem to get many of them excited. The first weekend, we set up game night. Charades was the choice of the night, and we had the attendees form their own groups. It was a blast. The following weekend, a live band performed as guests lounged around the fire pit. The week after that, we had bingo. Then after, card games. By the third month, we were barely getting guests to attend. I didn't understand why. I asked Cheryl and a few employees to see what they could uncover. The answer was simple - what we were setting up was not resonating with the guests. We had some frequent guests who explained that they had stopped going to other parks because the activities were not really why they were away from home. They just wanted somewhere to relax without any pressure. Games were the opposite of that because they demanded competition. Other guests were not fond of interacting with strangers, so they opted to stay in their RVs or lots whenever there were activities.

With the information, we pulled back on the games and only made them available for guests who wanted to borrow them to play with family members or other guests in their own time. We then focused on building a few more fire pits and adding more lounge chairs by the pool. We added a small library of used books and encouraged guests to donate any books they had. With this, I managed to carve out a niche for return guests - working and semi-retired RV owners looking for somewhere calm and quiet to unwind. This change in setup led to an uptick in guests who stayed for a week or more, which was a huge jump in occupancy for us. Well, I tried implementing the same concept in the second park I invested in, and it was a bust.

This is not a lesson in luck, but rather, a lesson in logic. Just because it worked in one park, or even several parks, it is not guaranteed to work in yours. The key to running a successful park is finding out what works for you, specifically, and doing it well. However, there are various aspects of the business that need optimal performance, including:

- **Hiring and Training Practices:** Your employees can make or break your business. From tardiness, absenteeism, and disinterest, to theft, employee behavior reflects on the business and the park's brand. How often have you seen a restaurant get negative reviews because of the server's attitude toward the client? RV parks are in the service industry, and no matter what role your employee plays, there needs to be sufficient training regarding relating to clients and a benchmark for measuring their performance. No matter how "obvious" the position may be, clearly outline each employee's duties and, where applicable, the roster for performing said duties. Ambiguity serves no one, and it will cause unprecedented problems down the line.

How do you find employees? Proper hiring practices - through ads, agencies, or referrals - allow you to properly vet the employees. Rushing to fill a position is not a good idea, and you're better off contracting the work until you find a reliable candidate. Also, you have to determine if your employees will be full-time or part-time, and if you're running a seasonal park, when and how you will recruit the additional staff to handle the increasing workload.

Who will train the successful candidates? Will there be a probation period? How will performance be reviewed?

You need to put proper hiring practices in place, especially if you won't be running the park yourself. Management needs to understand the policies you set in place, so ensure that they are clear, concise, and not open to misinterpretation.

- **Booking and Rent Collection:** Which booking sites will you be using? How will you link them to your website? Will you offer deals and incentives to those who book through your website? How you handle your park's booking saves you from unnecessary headaches, especially during peak seasons. And to keep problems at bay, you need to ensure that each lot is properly taken care of to avoid guests needing to switch to other lots and disrupting the schedules. Who will be responsible for bookings? You need to have a way of following up on who made the bookings, so having one employee be primarily responsible for bookings is a great idea.

How will guests pay for their stay? How about long-term guests? A well set up rent collection system allows you to keep track of your park's primary income. I suggest having a no-cash policy, if possible, to avoid the temptation that comes with large sums of cash lying around. If a guest prefers paying in cash, have a way of noting this electronically, for example, by having a system that records who received the money. This way, you can follow up in case of anything. Income from other avenues in the park should also be properly documented. For your long-term residents, implement a strict collection deadline and impose the necessary fees and fines in case of late payment or defaults. Additionally, you can offer certain incentives for early payment.

- **Check-ins and Check-outs:** Setting the check-in and out times to coincide with working hours is the obvious thing to do. However, some guests may arrive late, or some may need to leave early for whatever reason. Because of these possibilities, you need systems to care for these guests' needs. You can pass on these duties to security staff or have a specific employee on duty in the park.

If possible, you can have a soft check-in, where the guests receive the necessary information packets, but everything else is processed during regular office hours. Whichever system you choose, ensure it is a seamless experience for your guests because late check-ins and early check-outs mean that the guests may still be a little tired or in a hurry, so complicating this process may spoil your guests' experience, or at least be an inconvenience.

- **Assessment and Maintenance Schedules:** The park needs to be in top condition at all times, and this is only possible if you remain on top of things. You cannot wait for the grass to be overgrown before it is mowed, or for the drains to be blocked before you clear the trash. And, to keep everything working properly, you need to create a proper schedule that gives your employees a game plan of when to check on things, log their condition, and schedule maintenance. This includes lots, as they are your guests' place of residence.

By creating well-crafted schedules, employees don't have to guess what needs to be checked, and nothing will fall into the cracks. Even if you have a great memory, you are bound to overlook things sometimes. Make sure you use the proper tools and reminder systems to keep your park running like a well-oiled machine.

- **Repairs and Upgrades:** The purpose of scheduled assessment and maintenance is to keep you apprised of the condition of your park, its amenities, and machinery. Regular maintenance lets you see if everything is in top shape or if repairs need to be done. Is the concrete in one lot chipping? Are the toilets flushing correctly? Are the drains working as required? Are the amenities serving the guests' needs? Is the machinery outdated?

The maintenance logs highlight when to undertake repairs and upgrades. This way, you can set aside enough funds and shop for the best rates before undertaking the project. Emergency repairs and upgrades can be expensive, so it's best to carry them out as scheduled instead of waiting for the last possible moment.

- **Chain of Command:** Being a friendly boss who allows employees their autonomy is well and good, but your park needs a well-established hierarchy. This is not to show the employees who's the boss, but as a way of creating a system of accountability. Who will oversee the cleaning of shared areas and park to ensure that everything is being done on schedule? Who will be in charge of check-ins and check-outs and assign staff to take care of the guests? Who will ensure that there are enough information packets and essentials on hand? Who will ensure that payments are made promptly and that the records are well-kept?

A clear chain of command lets employees know who to turn to with their questions or requests, and who to refer guests to. If your park is small, you may be able to handle everything comfortably, but this may not be the case if the park grows or during the busy seasons. Learn to delegate and ensure your staff knows who to report to.

- **Financials:** Don't try to take shortcuts with your books. This bad habit will catch on, and you won't know when it will catch up to you. Keep your personal expenses away from your business books, and vice versa. Record everything, no matter how small. This way, you discover the leaks before they turn into gushes. As I worked to unravel Gerry's books after I'd taken over the park, I discovered how small sums contributed to the overall loss of income. Apparently, his wife used to take money from the safe to pay for groceries and other small payments. I don't know why, but I decided to find more of the receipts. In eight months, she'd gone from $20 and $10 bills to 100s. In one strange month, she'd used about $2,438. The purchases started simple, mainly essentials, and these slowly graduated to almost everything in their home, including appliances and clothes.

Record everything, no matter how small, and keep the personal expenses far away from the business. If you have to take out money from the business to pay for something personal, record it as an advance on your salary if you have one. If not, deduct it from your profit cut.

- **Professional Distance:** Maintaining a cordial relationship with your guests is a great idea, as the rapport gives you a chance to get to know them better. This also helps the guests feel at ease, and they will be more honest about their stay if they find you likable. However, you have to be careful not to get so close to your guests that it hinders your ability to conduct business properly. This is especially the case with long-term guests, as you can't avoid getting closer as you interact frequently. However, make sure to draw a clear boundary so that you don't find yourself jeopardizing your business.

How you choose to run your park will impact the success of your business, so you need to be actively involved even if you are not directly running the business. Many RV park owners have seen their businesses losing money even in high occupancy seasons because of theft and mismanagement by whoever was left in charge. No matter how much you trust your manager, make it a point to visit the park frequently to ensure that the reports you're receiving are accurate. While I have not been burned by people I have left in charge of the park, one of my partners had a harrowing experience when he bought his first park. He decided to retain the employees who'd been with the park before the sale, believing their understanding of the park would make them an asset. He didn't want to run the park just yet, as he had a few deals to wrap up on the other side of the country. He entrusted the park to the manager, and off he went. Two months in, the park's finances were worsening, but not significantly. The manager had an answer to every question, so there wasn't much he could do.

Four months in, he got the real story from an unlikely source. One of his acquaintances visited the park on a whim and was shocked by what he found. Only two staff members were on-site, and the manager had not been in the park for a few days. Overwhelmed, the employees had stopped putting in much work and only did what they could, which wasn't much. The park was about half filled, but most of the lots were cluttered and guests were using the adjacent empty lots as they pleased. The acquaintance took a pretty lengthy video and promptly sent it over. Enraged and feeling betrayed, my partner took the first flight and headed into the park. It took half a year to reverse the damage caused, and he was forced to look for a partner to help him with the park since he'd incurred too heavy a financial loss to remain the sole owner. And that's how I met Trent. His experience was enough to keep him cautious, and he's less trusting these days.

Don't let yourself slack off as an owner, even if your employees are high performers. Stay apprised of what's happening in the park, and ensure that major purchases can't be made without your authorization. Stay interested and invested in your park so you can fix issues sooner, not later. Otherwise, you may find yourself too deep into the red.

Chapter 9 - Marketing & Advertising Mastery

"Do what you do so well that they will want to see it again and bring their friends."

~ Walt Disney

With your park ready (or as ready as can be), you now need to find ways of getting guests to know that the park is ready for occupancy, and give them reasons to choose your park. Marketing and advertising your park is an essential part of the business, even if the park has been in existence for years. Fortunately, the internet and social media have made advertising campaigns less expensive, but this doesn't mean you can just put out anything. Also, the number of marketing options has increased, which means that your marketing expenses can quickly add up if you're not careful. Just throwing a bunch of darts at the board and hoping some stick is not the right way to do it.

Before you choose any advertisement and marketing option, you have to consider a few things:

What is your aim with the campaign? Not all marketing and advertising campaigns are the same. You may be looking for more guests as the general goal, but what are the specifics? Are you looking for more guests to book through your website, or are you hoping to make your brand more visible as the park is still new? Various goals will influence your ad content and medium differently, so you must be clear about your end goals.

How will you know if the campaign is successful or not? Defining clear goals is impressive and all that, but you need to have a way of analyzing the efficacy of your campaign. By clearly defining your Key Performance Indicators (KPIs), you can determine if the campaign is achieving its intended goals or not. Through analysis with the defined metrics as your yardstick, you get to see what part of the campaign is working, and better, you get to find opportunities that you'd previously overlooked.

What is the timeframe? There is no way you can run a particular campaign indefinitely, so you need to define the timeframe for each campaign clearly. If it works well, you have a foundation that you can build on for your next campaign. If the campaign does not achieve its intended goal, you learn from it and make changes accordingly. The concrete timeframe should be enough to give you the necessary feedback. However, you can ditch the campaign if it becomes clear it is not working from the onset. You must be flexible enough to change course as soon as possible to avoid losses. And if the campaign seems to be picking up steam as the deadline approaches, it may be best to give it a bit more time as you monitor its performance.

What will be the evaluation process? Who will be in charge of the evaluation? How often will this be done? What issues or opportunities do you expect from the campaign, and how will you recognize them? Running an ad is a somewhat intensive process, and you need to be well-prepared to handle its various aspects. The evaluation and analysis of each campaign should be carried out with intense focus, objectively, and consistently.

How much are you putting into your campaign? Your budget constraints also dictate which marketing campaign you undertake. Every ad campaign will incur a cost, no matter which form it takes. How much you pay, however, varies tremendously from one campaign to another. While social media can be relatively affordable, this doesn't mean that you throw money at it without considering why you are using it, or if it will offer the best value for your money. Have a concrete budget and a system for determining how much value the ad contributes to the business. This can be through various metrics, including cost per win, cost per lead, cost per conversion, or cost per click. If the financial return of your campaign is dismal or nonexistent, you need to reevaluate and find ways of optimizing the cost. A marketing campaign will increase your operating expenses, and the core focus should be finding a campaign that generates enough revenue to justify the costs incurred.

With all your ducks in a row, choose a campaign that matches your goals. For many people, social media marketing seems to be the go-to for all their marketing campaigns. However, you need to think carefully about how social media can work for you before you throw your ad into the void of ads that fill each platform. Most of the camps I choose to invest in cater to retirees and families. My worst-performing campaigns were the ones I ran on Instagram. The Facebook campaign, on the other hand, generated better leads and had more conversions overall. To be honest, the Instagram ad campaign was not my idea. One of my partners wanted to open up the park to more "hip" clientele, and I was entirely on board with the idea. A few hundred dollars later, I couldn't wait to pull out. I was frustrated since I didn't understand Instagram, and the social media manager we hired was not really up to the task. The engagement was dismal, and inquiries were handled poorly. So, maybe it was not the platform itself, but I still chose to stick with what I knew. We have Instagram pages that are updated frequently, as they provide direct links to our website. Plus, our guests get to tag us in their pictures, increasing our engagement.

Let's explore some marketing tools at your disposal, but remember that these are not all supposed to be embarked on at the same time or all at once. As a park owner, your understanding of your business and goals determines the methods that best align with your long-term and short-term goals. Don't jump on the bandwagon of the "trendy" marketing tool without understanding what it entails. For example, if your park is in a remote location and does not have glamping capabilities, using a luxury lifestyle influencer is not a great option. The most significant factor determining your ad campaign is **who you want to attract.**

- **Direct Mail Services:** This is a great option for your park, but you have to be careful about what you include in your emails. Just writing emails to your clients is well and good, but it's easy to cross into the annoying spammy section if you're not careful. Collecting emails from guests who visit the park or your website is a great way to start the mailing list. Some people buy data from third-party companies, and you may also choose to do this. However, because I hate receiving emails from places I don't know, or I've never heard of, I spare my potential guests this horror.

When I started sending out emails, I'd just put random information about the park, then include links to the website and other social media platforms. However, after attending a seminar about client retention, my emails changed. Now, I send out well-curated newsletters that span two to three pages. The newsletter is sent out quarterly, as the new season approaches. The first page includes a summary of important information, like the season's offers, any changes to the park, and updates about any contests run in the previous season. The other two pages offer more details and always have pictures of the guests and links to our website. I love pictures, so the newsletters are picture heavy and never take more than five minutes to read. This system has worked well for me, and it's usually pretty simple to hire a freelancer to put my ideas into a workable format to send out.

Direct mail service can be a formidable weapon if it is wielded well, and you need to learn how to do it. First, ensure that the recipients can opt out of the mailing service without hassle. Make it easy to sign up for the newsletter and easy to opt-out. When it comes to the information shared, ensure it is relevant and well-written. No one wants to read a poorly written email with typos and unnecessary information. Also, make sure that you include the necessary links, with minimal navigation. For example, if your email is about new offers at the park, the link should go straight to the offers page, not the landing page. This way, the recipient finds what they are looking for relatively easy, making their experience seamless and satisfying. You also need to send in your emails with relative frequency, but don't bombard recipients with too many emails in a short time. A monthly newsletter works well, but I settled on three months because I intended to use the newsletter to update guests on upcoming offers and incentives.

- **Partnerships and Events:** Your local community is a great place to build up your brand, especially if you can offer incentives and other perks to local guests looking for a place to escape their daily grind. By partnering with local businesses, like restaurants and grocery stores, you get to form a mutually beneficial relationship that will foster the growth of your park. If you don't have a restaurant or store in your park, having the local businesses supply these goods to your campground is a great idea, as it allows your guests to spend time in the park without having to leave to buy what they need. Additionally, local businesses may be willing to offer you discounts, distribute flyers, or carry brochures advertising your park and any offers you have.

If you can spare a few dollars, sponsor a few local events to give your park the exposure it needs. Because these events will be posted online, your campground will be featured, and if you can have them link your social media pages or websites, the better.

Partnerships with RV dealerships is a great idea if you want to attract more guests. Because the dealers are already in the industry, having them "talk up" your campground can be a great way to boost your occupancy. You can have perks and incentives in brochures, flyers, or information packets available at the dealerships.

Word of caution, though. As you enter these partnerships, ensure there is something in it for you. Don't be on the losing end of the deal, as the aim of these partnerships and sponsorships is to foster a mutually beneficial relationship. Always remember that you are running a business, and no matter how altruistic you may want to be, your business won't survive on altruism. A little selfishness goes a long way.

- **Online Directories:** Search engines like Google, Superpages, Google Places, Abaco Small Business, and Bing have directories, and whether you like it or not, your business will be in their system. So, why not let this work for you? By claiming your listing, you can add relevant information regarding your park, including your working hours, contact information, and links to your website.

Ads on search engines are also a great way to gain visibility on your site when the relevant keywords are searched. If your marketing budget allows, you can consider this option.

- **Social Media Campaigns, Content, and Engagement:** Social media marketing campaigns are more than just creating and boosting a post. Your ad is an extension of your social media presence. The ad is supposed to complement your pages, which need content matching the goals you hope to achieve with every marketing campaign. Have you ever clicked on the profile of an ad and found yourself on a page that seemingly has no rhyme or reason? It's frustrating, and gives off a "scammy" vibe. Your business pages should differ from your personal accounts, and you need to meticulously curate your page to showcase your campground's strengths. Your posts should feature the right hashtags, well-written captions, and beautiful pictures. If possible, invest in a great camera for the park. Your bio should include the necessary information, including contacts and links to your website. If you're running ads, ensure that the link works and directs to the relevant page.

Additionally, you need to use the page to engage with commenters. Tag clients if you post their pictures on the site, showcase your employees' strengths, and ensure that events are posted on the page. Contests, offers, and perks should be showcased on the site, with working links if you need to redirect the visitors to the relevant page. Always check that the links redirect to the correct page to avoid frustrating your visitors.

Scheduling your posts using tools like Hootsuite, Buffer, Sendible, Zoho Social, and other alternatives allows you to consistently post on your page, which is great for your visibility. This also allows you to curate content according to themes and properly think about what you post, instead of posting random things that may make your page seem disorganized.

- **Website, Blogs, and Review Sites:** This goes without saying, but if you choose to have a website, you need to put in the work to ensure that the experience will be seamless for anyone visiting it. Optimize your landing page to ensure the information is well-presented, relevant, and eye-catching. The landing page will keep the visitor interested, as it is your park's first impression. Additionally, the navigation pane should be visible, with the common links placed first. For your park, the navigation to the booking page should be clear and easy to find. Your contact information should also be visible, and so should a map of the park. Your website is a great marketing tool because it will be linked to your social media pages and any online marketing campaign. Because traffic is meant to be directed to the website, make sure that pages load fast, and that your website is well-curated for a mobile-friendly experience.

A blog on your website is a great way to make Search Engine Optimization work for you. With blogs, you can use long-form keywords naturally, which makes it easier for your website to rank better. However, ensure that your blog posts are well-written, relevant, informative and, most of all, interesting. Even if it is a short post explaining your site's booking process, highlighting an event, or explaining an aspect of RV life, your blog works for you on other social media platforms and can be incorporated into your direct mail services.

Reviews are a great way of getting feedback about your park, and present an opportunity for better engagement with your guests. Google, Good Sam, RVBuddy, Campedium, Yelp, etc., will offer your guests a chance to highlight their experience in your park. While some reviews may be less than appealing, you need to take the opportunity presented by these sites - communicating with the guests. If you haven't yet, claim your business on these sites, and thank the reviewers. Engage them politely and cordially, even if you don't like what they say. Encourage your guests to leave reviews and thank them for doing so. Their honesty will clue you in on what you need to do to improve your park. The reviews also help your brand visibility, but unfortunately, this can also fall on the negative side. So, ensure you deliver what your park promises, and your guests will play a greater role in your marketing campaign.

- **Membership Affiliations:** Affiliate programs, especially if your park is new and has yet to build its client base, can be a great way to give your park the exposure it needs while still earning income. Programs like Good Sam, RVnGo, RV Life, LightStream, Camping World, RV America Insurance, and Outdoorsy offer affiliate memberships to various parks, and it would be a great idea to check their terms and what you need to do to qualify. While you may not get the full price for your lot with these programs, the commissions and exposure may be great for your park in the long run.

Keep in mind that the terms of these programs vary, so you need to take your time with the research to ensure that your choice will benefit you. By having your park's name on the list of affiliates, guests with these memberships may accord you the same trust they accord the program, and if their stay is satisfactory, they will also help your campground attract more guests. By hopping on the program's reputation, the work you need to put in to shine a spotlight on your brand gets a bit lighter.

- **Traditional Ad Campaigns:** Local ad campaigns can still work, especially in local and niche publications. Some campground magazines offer ad space; if you can afford to include your campground, please do. However, be sure to choose local or state magazines, as guests will always be more willing to take a chance on you if you are relatively close as opposed to hundreds or thousands of miles away.

This list is by no means exhaustive, and you need to take time to ensure that whichever choice you make aligns with your goals, client demographic, and that you can deliver what is promised in the marketing material. No matter what you do, never promise what you can't deliver, as this sets you up for failure as a business owner. Your pictures on websites and social media pages should reflect the true state of your park, and if you don't like how it looks, work on improving the park. Don't draw guests in with false promises because even if you don't have a well-established online presence, your business will still be visible online.

Final word - no matter what marketing campaign you choose, start small. Try out the option and analyze its efficacy before you commit to a higher level. If an ad is not working for your chosen demographic, don't try to widen the net. Work on fixing the issues or finding better avenues to reach your target market. And finally, never stop trying. Marketing will last through the park's lifetime, so don't get tired of creating new campaigns to try out.

Chapter 10 - Features of The Most Successful Campgrounds

"Success doesn't come from what you do occasionally, it comes from what you do consistently."

~ Marie Forleo

Success, even in the RV industry, can mean different things to different people. However, because your park is, at its core, a business venture, you have to incorporate the mainstream metrics to determine if your park is successful or not. For the longest time, I would only focus on the bottom line to determine if my park was successful or not. The focus on improving amenities, increasing income, and reducing costs would occupy me endlessly. I had cut a few corners to reduce expenses, but this proved to be a stupid move on my part. My biggest regret is choosing the cheapest developer for my first website. All I got was a rudimentary system that still relied on phone calls and emails for booking and booking confirmations. This was okay for a while, but guests were finding it easier to book with competitors, and they chose to embrace the easier option. In the end, I still had to hire another developer to create what I had passed on the first time, and this time the rates had gone up significantly because demand had spiked. As a result, I prefer getting top-notch service and paying the premium to ensure I have the best experience. This has forced me to use my personal funds for the business, but I always log that as an investment that will be recouped in time. Throughout my time as a campground owner, my metrics for success have shifted and changed, but the following have always been part of my checklist:

Return on Investment (ROI): As a business, your success will always be measured fiscally whether you like it or not. While you may have chosen to invest in your RV park because you love the work, you still have to create value with it. If you have a negative or low ROI, you may be doing something wrong, or you need to revamp your practices. A high ROI is a great measure of your success, as it shows the value you have created with the business since you bought, built, or invested in it.

Personnel: Your park employees are the backbone of the business. They are the people entrusted to turn your vision into reality by maintaining the park, helping customers, and ensuring everything runs smoothly. Because of this, you need to ensure that you have a low turnover rate and your employees are performing at peak capacity without running them haggard. This means a decent wage, appropriate time off, well-defined and structured roles, and well-structured schedules. Always ensure that benefits are well outlined and premiums are paid on time. If there are deductibles, ensure these are remitted on time to avoid complicating the employees' lives. If you provide accommodation and/or meals, ensure that the living spaces are well maintained, have the necessary amenities, and that meals are healthy and nutritionally balanced.

Performance reviews should be conducted regularly, and a conflict resolution system should be established. I feel successful if my employees are satisfied and I have no frequent turnovers. Because great help is sometimes hard to come by, I always ensure that I do my best to retain the talent that lands in my park. If employees have ideas, hear them out. By giving them the space to contribute to the park, you show them they matter. Employee satisfaction is made up of more than competitive wages.

Marketing Strategies: Are your marketing strategies having the desired impact? If your marketing campaigns are achieving the goals and targets set, you do have a successful camp. Hitting the mark with your campaigns means that you have found your target market and are capitalizing on your niche base. Keep it up.

State of Amenities: Are the lots, equipment, shared rooms, and amenities functioning as they should? Are you up to date on your maintenance and repair schedules? Is everything clean, neat, and ready for use? You are allowed to have a few faulty items in the park, but this should not last for long. If you are running haggard fixing things every day, or if employees have to be frequently pulled from their set schedules to work on an emergency, you need to evaluate your operations. Emergencies should be few and far between, as your schedules must incorporate every aspect of the park. The more amenities there are, the more complex this may be. However, you need to find a system that keeps you on top of everything in the park. If you never seem to handle everything on time, consider adding more employees or reducing the amenities in the park. The goal is to provide exceptional service, not cram everything into the park and get overwhelmed.

Quality of Service: This ties in with the previous aspects of the business, as the quality of service is usually a byproduct of the management, operation, and personnel decisions you make. However, it doesn't hurt to have your employees enroll in training programs that will give them the skills to provide exceptional service to clients. Even small changes like better uniforms and neat working spaces can add to the exemplary quality of service. If you have a restaurant or offer delivery services, food presentation, speed of delivery, and straightforward resolution of issues can go a long way.

Customer Satisfaction: Is your park customer-centric, or do you treat them as a money-making project? I know of one park owner who had tip jars almost everywhere in the park and encouraged employees to accept tips for services rendered; it was almost unbearable to watch. I'd stopped by to visit, and even though the park was clean and everything was well run, I hated seeing the jars everywhere. Some employees would rush to help just to put out a hand for a tip. I understand why the owner put up the jars in the first place, but he quickly went overboard.

Customer satisfaction is a valuable aspect of the business, as it will help generate more business and solidify your brand in the market. However, in pursuing great service, adopt services and programs that match your customer niche. Encourage your guests to leave reviews, but don't push them too hard.

Feedback Incorporation: It's one thing to encourage guests and employees to share their thoughts and suggestions, and an entirely different thing to find ways of incorporating these ideas successfully. How will you handle the feedback you get? Do you blindly follow suggestions you deem great? Do you check on the viability of the ideas? Or do you ignore anything that's not your idea?

I have a book of ideas, contributed by guests and employees alike. With management, we sit and whittle out the outrageous ideas before including the employees in a discussion to determine if the other ideas are worth it. In one of the parks I owned, the layout seemed simple to us, but apparently, guests were having difficulty figuring out where some lots were because of the unconventional design. When a guest suggested adding signage, we liked the idea. However, because these would require maintenance, we had to involve the employees to find a cost-efficient method. The old unused RV in one corner of the park found its use. The metal and other parts were repurposed into one of the most fabulous lot signage I've ever seen.

Not all ideas are great, but you need to be open to diving into the murk to find the gold. And if you can, find a great way of rewarding the person behind the idea. For my employees, I always try to give cash gifts or cash equivalents. For guests, a mention in the newsletter and merchandise or discounts are the rewards for any implemented idea. I usually ask them which they prefer, and sometimes I issue gift cards if their location is too expensive to deliver merch to.

Safety Procedures: You need to ensure that your park is safe. Investing in the best insurance policy is half the battle, as you have to prevent injury and damage to people and property. Are there fire extinguishers in the park? The correct ones? What is your evacuation policy? Are the emergency numbers well-displayed or easy to access? Are your employees well-versed in first aid? Do they get frequent retraining? Sometimes this may seem excessive, but you must be committed to keeping everyone in your park safe. Your response in times of tragedy also affects your brand, and you don't want to destroy your business because of a shoddy response.

Take proper care of equipment and your park, and ensure guests know what to do in an emergency.

Value for Money: This applies to both your business and the guests. As you price your accommodation and other services, ensure that you don't set your prices too high or too low. Finding the right balance might be difficult, but by looking at it from a customer's perspective, you will be able to find the right balance. If you will be charging for the activities at the park, ensure that the guests get a better price than the day visitors. This way, your guests feel the value of staying with you. You and your guest should be left feeling that each dollar was well-earned and well-spent, respectively.

Ease of Booking: Don't give your competition a chance to snag your guest. Create a seamless and automated booking system with clear cancellation policies. Your payment protocols should be well set and secure, and you need to have a well-established dispute resolution policy. When guests know what to expect, they put their trust in you. Make it easy for your guests to find and stay with you.

Customer Engagement: Your contact information must be well placed on your website and social media pages, and you need a great response time. You need to have one employee handle your communication, and if this is not possible, ensure that those who help have impeccable customer service skills. Generic responses turn off clients, so you need to invest in proper training for the employee handling correspondence. This way, you get to form a kinship with existing and potential guests. However, maintain professionalism at all times, and refrain from using your business accounts to discuss personal matters.

The above metrics are by no means exhaustive. They are the first things I analyze in my parks before considering other factors that may be unique to the park. Success is more than just money, and this will be reflected in your park's ability to retain guests and employees, and in how efficient its operation is.

Chapter 11 – Taking it to the Next Level, Expanding to More Parks, & More!

"Growth is a spiral process, doubling back on itself, reassessing, and regrouping."

~ Julia Margaret Cameron

Once your park is up and running, you cannot sit back and just let things be as they are. There are always ways to improve, innovate, and grow; finding ways to run more efficiently should be your goal. Scaling a business is something that needs to be done. With your park now running as it should, you have the time to identify any redundancies, excess expenses, and unnecessary strains. In one park I visited, the owner was hell-bent on keeping his employees mowing with walk-along mowers, not realizing that it was taking a chunk of time that would have been better focused on more productive activities. Mowing would take almost a week to complete, and three employees had to be fully involved while two more helped out for a few hours. He was doing this to "save" money, which was absurd. I finally had the chance to buy out the park four years later, and the first thing I did was get a riding mower. With this, only two employees were needed on mowing duty, while the other three could focus on other aspects of the park.

Whenever I have a park running, I check on redundancies to ensure that I am not spending more than I need to. Every employee has a well-defined list of duties and responsibilities, and if they get overwhelmed, we restructure to ease the burden. The constant monitoring, reviews, and restructures are frustrating and chaotic, but in the end, there are fewer expenses because everything is optimized. Scaling is an integral part of your success as a park owner, and in the RV park industry, there are various ways you can choose to make your business profitable while providing top-notch service.

- **Meter subletting:** This may not be possible for your short-stay clients, but it is a viable option for your extended-stay or permanent guests. By having the guest cater for their own sewer, water, and/or trash disposal costs, you can save on expenses. Because they are billed for what they use, guests will be more conscientious about how they use the amenities, which often translates to lower costs for the park owner.

- **Storage Services:** One park owner decided to complete his parks in phases, as he didn't want more than 100 lots in a single phase. Each development was to run like a separate entity, with only a few shared features for all phases. The four-phase project stalled after phase two, and he spent months figuring out what to do. In a stroke of luck, a few guests wondered whether he could offer storage for their RVs and boats. The park was near a lake, and some guests were not fond of hiring boats every summer. The group of friends had spent time looking for a storage rental near other RV parks, to no avail. This was the idea the park owner needed. He promised to look into it, and managed to build a massive structure with units to hold the boats. What started as an operation with five boats quickly turned into an RV and motorhome storage yard. A few years later, he began reselling RVs and motorhomes from the same lot. Needless to say, phases three and four never materialized.

If you have space in your park, you can consider setting up storage units. You don't have to store boats and motorhomes, though. With storage rentals, like many businesses, you need to find what your potential customers need.

- **RV Resale and Rentals:** I don't have the heart for this, but I have referred quite a few guests to other park owners who offer these services. When one of my friends was selling his park, he used my park as his base of operations for a while. Basically, he used empty lots in his park to store the RVs he was either renting or selling. When they were in the lot, he would also rent them out to guests staying in the park. The RVs were earning money whether parked or on the road. Because he rented them out also, many of his renters turned into buying clients a few months or years down the line.

He invested his time in ensuring that the RVs were in top shape, ran smoothly, and worked properly. He'd offer his buyers a discounted accommodation fee if they chose to stay at the park for a few days to get the feel of the RVs first. This built trust in him, as he would allow you to choose a different RV if the one you were looking at didn't live up to your expectations. Because of this, he had to segue into full-time RV rentals and sales. The demand was so high he'd barely had time to take care of the park. In the end, he built a small 20-lot park/RV yard.

As an RV park owner, adding rental or resale to your portfolio is a great idea because you understand the market, and your guests are all potential clients. However, you have to understand that this side of the business has its own set of challenges and risks, so you need to be well prepared.

- **Large Vehicle Wash:** Most RV parks, yours included, have a rule banning guests from washing their RVs in the park. This is because the runoff water tends to pool in certain areas, and it is a waste of water. With a large vehicle wash, you get to provide professional service to your guests, and, depending on the location of the car wash, other passing vehicles. This may be incredibly profitable in areas with high RV traffic, like resort locations. For the guests at your park, you can offer discounted prices or other perks if they get their vehicles washed at your establishment.

- **Park Expansion and Purchase:** If you find your footing as an RV park owner and find the work satisfying, you can choose to expand your park if you have the space or buy new parks to add to your portfolio. However, you have to ensure that the management and operation of your parks are solid before owning and operating other parks. I know a few owners of three to four parks, and for a while, I had two parks before I decided to sell one.

Park expansion has always been my go-to scaling strategy, but this rarely involves adding lots. Instead, I usually add other amenity features or services. One park had a game room since most guests had teenagers. I built a simple hall, added partitions for three or more people, and set up a few arcade games. One wall was used to project games on some competition nights. I charged for the games, but the competitions were for the fun of it. The popularity of this park with teens and preteens meant full occupancy during holidays. Finally, I bit the bullet and added a few more lots. I sold the park two years later, and now it has a waterpark and "disco" setup with nonalcoholic drinks and bonfire parties.

- **Park Investment:** Lately, I have been opting for owning a part of a park instead of the entire thing. I am a silent partner in four parks, and I love that I am not involved in the daily operation. If you find that running a park is not for you but still want to be in the RV park business, investing can be a great option. However, always ensure that you do your due diligence. Don't put your money in a sinking ship.

There are many more ways to scale your business, and the ones listed above are the ones I've personally had experience with. I know park owners who launched websites to help other owners connect with specialized services at economical prices, others who sell customizable booking sites, and others who offer merch creation services at great prices for park owners. There is so much you can do if you have the time and interest, but you have to remember that if you are still at the helm of the park, that is your priority. Your search for bigger and greater should not come at the expense of your core business.

Made in the USA
Columbia, SC
20 April 2025